GOSSIP

FROM ACROSS THE

POND

Articles Published in the United Kingdom's
Gay and Lesbian Humanist

1996 - 2005

By

WARREN ALLEN SMITH

Published by chelCpress
31 Jane Street (10-D)
New York, NY 10011
warrenallensmith@gmail.com

Smith, Warren Allen
   Gossip From Across the Pond, Articles Published in the United Kingdom's Gay and Lesbian Humanist, 1996 – 2005

1. Gossip, Gay 2. Paul Cadmus 3. Royston Ellis
4. Bon Soir 5. Gay in the 1960s 6. *Gay & Lesbian Humanist* 6. Gay and Lesbian History 7. Gay Humanists

ISBN-978-0-557-55155-2

Second Printing
Printed in the United States of America

Photo of the *Queen Mary 2*'s Maiden Voyage to Manhattan, by Warren Allen Smith. Other Photos Courtesy of Google Images.

Contents

INTRODUCTION

Warren Allen Smith has written for *Gay and Lesbian Humanist* since 1996.

In the 1950s he was Book Review Editor of *The Humanist*, an American secular publication then published in Yellow Springs, Ohio, now published in Washington, D.C.

He is author of *Who's Who in Hell* (Barricade Books, 2000), which was reviewed by George Broadhead in the Autumn 2000 issue of *Gay and Lesbian Humanist*. Also, he is author of *Celebrities in Hell* (Barricade Books, 2002).

"Hell," he describes in both books, is a theological invention. It does not physically exist. It is an imaginary place that has little or no significance to the philosophic naturalist, whose focus (instead of being good in this life as a way to spend eternity with God the Creator) is entirely humanistic (seeking pleasure and avoiding pain; finding personal development through enlightenment; achieving peace of mind; developing ethically; and constructing a non-supernaturalistic view of human life based upon logic and the scientific method of reasoning).

Smith's interest in gossip dates back to his hearing on radio and reading in newspapers material by the inventor of gossip columns, **Walter Winchell** (1897-1972). That widely quoted commentator was known for starting, "Good evening, Mr. and Mrs

America, and all the ships at sea." For Smith, who was raised in a dull Iowa town of 328 people, it was fascinating to hear what was happening in café society from a person who obtained tips about what people were doing by sitting with his typewriter at Manhattan's Stork Club.

In 1944, Smith led his company onto Normandy's Omaha Beach. In 1961 he founded Variety Recording Studio with **Fernando Rodolfo de Jesus Vargas Zamora**, a Costa Rican who would be his companion for 40 years – they recorded Liza Minnelli's first demo, with Marvin Hamlisch on the piano, to name but two of their illustrious clients. In 1969 Smith was a veteran of the Stonewall Rebellion. In 1989, Vargas died of K-S. In 2001 from his windows Smith watched as Muhammad Atta brought down the World Trade Towers.

Smith, 88, writes on his iMac computer from Greenwich Village, New York. His website: http://wasm.us

Autumn 1996

[Column, "Scene from New York," was written under the pseudonym of Allen Windsor.]

When **Gore Vidal** was elected a Humanist Laureate by others in the International Academy of Humanism, he overlooked the vote, failing to acknowledge the honour from the Council for Secular Humanism.

The Academy of Humanism's 75 members, who are listed in issues of *Free Inquiry*, a journal of the Council for Secular Humanism in Buffalo, New York, include five Nobel Prize winners and such familiar GALHA names as Sir **Hermann Bondi** and Professor **Rob Tielman**.

The inaction by the author of *Myra Breckenridge* was not particularly surprising. He had, years ago, deliberately refused membership in the prestigious 250-member **American Academy of Arts and Letters**, telling them, "Thanks, but I already belong to the Diners Club."

Also, he has piqued some noted people with his acerbic opinions: Of **Solzhenitsyn**: "He is a bad novelist and a fool. The combination usually makes for great popularity in the United States." Of **Ronald Reagan**: "A triumph of the embalmer's art." Of **Truman Capote**: "Capote has made lying an art. A mini art." Of America: "The civilization whose absence drove **Henry James** to Europe."

Vidal's *Live From Golgotha* (1982) was a satire as blasphemous as anything **Salman Rushdie** might imagine. Its **Bishop of**

Ephesus, the heterosexual **Timothy** who was said to have had "the largest dick in our part of Asia Minor," was represented as having been an acolyte and "love toy" of **St. Paul**. Vidal's non-theistic bent was never hidden, as exemplified by a 1992 declaration, "I'm really interested now in trying to destroy monotheism in the United States. That is the source of all the problems."

In 1995 his autobiographical *Palimpsest* (1995) pulled no punches and included tales showing he knew almost everybody who was "anybody." It included in Vidalian detail his homosexual experiences (never a bottom); his one love (**Jimmy Trimble**, a Marine scout killed by a grenade in 1944); **Gene Vidal** (Gore said of his father, who was in medical books because he had three balls, "I never dared look - you don't look at parents - but it is recorded that they were all of equal size"); **Greta Garbo** (told she should return to Sweden, that the king was dying, responded, "So far to go, and for what? He'll die anyway"); **Wallis Simpson** (who died after an anesthetic following a fifth face-lift); the **Duke of Windsor** (Wallis "knew how to control his premature ejaculation"); **Eleanore Roosevelt** (known for serving "the most inedible meals in the White House"); **Paul Newman** (who, when reading **Nietzsche** aboard a troopship, found a chaplain making a pass at him and it really put him off. "Off Christianity or homosexuality?" Vidal had asked. "Neither," responded Newman. "Nietzsche"); **Jackie Onassis**'s losing her virginity (to **John Marquand Jr.** on a creaky Parisian lift); **Lee Radzwill** (who put messages in Pres. Kennedy's coffin, "presumably for Jack to deliver on the other side"); **President Kennedy** (**Tennessee Williams** told Gore he found Kennedy's ass "attractive," to which Kennedy, when told, grinned, "That's very exciting."). The book has dishy tales about dozens of others whom Vidal knew personally, many intimately.

A pity, then, that such an outspokenly colorful atheist had ignored the Academy of Humanism honor!
So, a mentor of the Council, I came up with a fey plan to get Vidal into the Humanist Academy. *Palimpsest* had cited his affection for pre-Judeo-Christian times and specifically for **Apuleius**, **Petronius**, and **Lucretius**. It was the latter who, he found, had anticipated Darwin by 2000 years. Mortals were not let down from on high by some golden chain, Lucretius held. To

8

which Vidal declared, "So much for the antique notion of **Cadmus** sowing dragon's teeth to create human beings or the peculiarly silly story of **Adam and Eve** believed by so many of my countrymen." Further, it was Lucretius who was "aware - how, I wonder - that we evolved."

Taking an envelope which contained a copy of my *Free Inquiry* interview with **Sir Peter Ustinov**, and including inside a self-addressed stamped envelope with an unsigned memo, "I agree to be listed as a Humanist Laureate." I hiked off to a local book-signing.

"Mr. Vidal," I said as I approached the 70-year-old, somewhat dourly, "you and I," and here my voice raised in volume," are in love with the same man!"

It was clear from his reaction that he had never before seen me. For a split second, he seemed both startled and bemused. Observers anticipated a scene. Side conversations abruptly halted. A Random House representative approached, warily. Vidal clearly was trying to guess what was about to happen.

I then slipped him the envelope.

"Lucretius," I said with a smile.

My next day's mail included the memo . . . signed.

Winter 1996

[Allen Windsor Reports from the Big Apple.]

Edward Albee, the American playwright who is openly gay but who dislikes being called an American gay playwright, spoke on Dec. 10th to several hundred at the Gay Center in Manhattan. Two days prior, he had received the 1996 Kennedy Center Honors Award from **President and Mrs. Bill Clinton** at the White House.

Arriving in New York to applause although a few minutes late, he headed straight for the men's room at the front of the room, then received tumultuous applause upon exiting. In an off-the-cuff, very informal session, he gave no lecture but answered anyone's questions. Asked to dish the White House event, he said the best part was that he was the honoree, that he didn't have to "do" anything. Did his lover go along? Oh, yes, and for decades he has always been accompanied by whomever his current lover had been. How was the food? The cold shrimp was marvelous. Did he get to speak to the prez? Well, he got in a few licks on behalf of Federal aid to the arts. Had he written *The Zoo Story* in four weeks? Yes, while earning $37 per week at Western Union, using a company typewriter and paper he purloined. When did he realize he was gay? Well, he was in a prep school at the age of 12. Is he an unbeliever who, like so many gays, does not believe in an afterlife? Well, no. **Jesus** was a good revolutionary, although Albee didn't go along with the divinity part. In fact, he had startled a lady when recently asked what person, if he could have dinner with anyone, he would choose. He had answered Jesus. "Well," he told the attentive gay crowd, "who did you think I'd have chosen, **Neil Simon**?"

No mention was made that **Salman Rushdie**, when he performed as an actor on Pakistani TV in Albee's *The Zoo Story*, had had to cut a line about God's being a colored queen who wears a kimono and plucks His eyebrows.

Albee has consistently denied that he originally had two gays in mind rather than the straight couple in *Who's Afraid of Virginia Woolf* (1962; film, 1966). Asked again, he explained that the plot would not make sense in light of the couple's fixation about a nonexistent son whom they had created to sustain themselves in their attempt, they said, to "try to claw our way into compassion." How could two males have had a son? Besides, he observed, "I know a woman from a man. If I'd had males in mind, I would say so."

Although **David Tribe**, the Australian-born secularist, has termed Albee a nonbeliever, Albee made it clear that he thinks Jesus lived, likes his outlook and character, but just doesn't accept all that divinity stuff. Albee may never even have heard about secular humanists, in short. **Gore Vidal**, on the contrary, is a total nonbeliever.

.

New Yorkers are not booking wedding packages to Honolulu. Not just yet. Honolulu may hope to become the Reno of gay marriages, but each of the 50 state legislatures makes its own marriage rules. There are 29 states that let first cousins marry and 21 that don't. In some, females can marry at 15, whereas in most others they must be 18. Already, 16 states have passed laws banning same-sex marriage and 20 have rejected such laws. Although gays may eventually be allowed to marry, it will be years and waves of backlash before all the legal issues are resolved. Anyone for a really long engagement?

.

Angel Garcia, a licensed groom, was interrupted about midnight by a security officer at the NY Aqueduct race track. Naked, he was lying on the stall floor, apparently having fallen off the plastic bucket he had been standing on. The filly, Saratoga Capers, was chained and, after it was examined by a vet, Garcia was charged with engaging in sexual conduct with an animal. News reports did not suggest whether Garcia was gay or a breeder. Meanwhile, in her first race since the incident, Saratoga Capers came in third, paying $3.10 on a $2. bet.

.

New York City's back rooms, pitch dark places which are packed to the four walls with guys of all shapes and sizes, have disappeared, to the credit of the much disliked Mayor **Rudy Giuliani**. Responsible gay leaders have hailed their closing, claiming it was shocking that condom-less sex had been so common at a time when gays have been leaders in educating the general public about avoiding venereal and HIV problems. At the November 1996 Humanist World Congress held in Mexico City, at least four humanists were so intrigued that several gay bars openly had back rooms that they spent part of the conference "observing" orgies in the darkness.

.

No gay humanist group in Manhattan is on the World Wide Web. However, if you've a big hard disk, cruise over to http://www.gaycenter.org

Or if you want to pick up a nude Hawaiian,
http://www.douglassimonson.com/

Or for Costa Ricans,
http://www.indiana.edu/~arenal/

Spring 1997

Results from what gossip columnist **Bruce Bibby** calls the Annual Gay Superbowl, the telecast most call Oscar Night, are in. Sorry, but you already know there are few winners to report! My personal winner was in the audience. No, definitely not the Scientologist, **Tom Cruise**. My winner was the basketball player with Edwardian jacket and hat that covered his yellow hair, the lover who had enthralled Madonna for a few bedroom bouts, the controversial chap with tattoos who soon will appear in a movie: **Dennis Rodman**.

The English Patient, which was about a hero who turned British military secrets over to the Nazis in exchange for an airplane with which to rescue his mistress, was a winner. But not, of course, because it depicted **Peter Rühring** playing a British mapmaker in love with a young Moroccan man.

The Birdcage, the main movie with a gay plot but with no openly gay actors, at least had Oscar-nominated sets which were openly gay.

Romeo and Juliet featured Romeo's best friend, Mercutio, as a cross-dresser and a homosexual, but Mercutio won no award.

Playwright **Terrence McNally** said of *Hamlet* that "the greatest gay character ever written is Hamlet. . . . Reconsider his misogynic treatment of both his mother and his alleged girlfriend, reexamine his relationship with his best friend, Horatio, and check out his over-the-top enthusiasm for the theater and actors. If it takes one to know one, Hamlet is one. Trust me on this."

Marvin's Room was written by gay playwright **Scott McPherson** before he died of AIDS, and it had been hoped to have been a winner.

The Portrait of a Lady was based on a **Henry James** work. Henry's sister Alice was, according to **A. L. Rowse**, "a Lesbian of a pronounced type." **Will Self** in *Cock and Bull* (1992) thought

Henry had "only half a cock," having lost it chasing after a fire engine while trying to help an amateur fire fighter. Recent gay rumors link James to **Oliver Wendell Holmes**. But the movie, alas, was a portrait of **Isabel Archer**, not of the closeted Henry.

Fly Away Home was produced by gay Hollywood manager **Sandy Gallin**.

Michael Collins was a political drama produced by Geffen Pictures, which is headed by gay mogul **David Geffen**.

The First Wives Club's **Marc Shaiman** was nominated for best original musical or comedy score. And gay honcho **Scott Rudin** had produced the work which was reportedly scripted in part by reigning gay wit **Paul Rudnick**.

Shine depicts the Australian piano prodigy **David Helfgott**'s first teacher, played by **Nicholas Bell**. Helfgott's father always had wondered why the teacher had never married, and he found out when at one of David's concerts the teacher attended with a male date.

Sling Blade was about **Billy Bob Thornton**'s real-life pal **John Ritter**, a small-town gay everyman, the best-conceived gay character of the year, whose unconditional love extends to the woman he never bedded and the son he never fathered.

Gay characters in Hollywood movies are almost always played by non-gays. For example, by breeders such as **Antonio Banderas**; **Cher**; **Robert Downey Jr.**; **Whoopi Goldberg**; **Tom Hanks**; **Mariel Hemingway**; **Jonathan Pryce**; **Will Smith**; **Wesley Snipes**; **Terence Stamp**; **Patrick Stewart**; **Meryl Streep**; **Patrick Swayze**; **Uma Thurman**; **Jennifer Tilly**; and **Robin Williams**.

The gay **Sir Ian McKellen** predicted not long ago that "the first young actor of talent who comes out and stars in a movie and is a hit will be the most famous actor in the world and make a fortune for his agents and his managers and producers and the studio." Well, we who watch the Annual Gay Superbowl are still on hold and waiting!

Summer 1997

New Yorkers are abuzz about the flamboyantly gay character, Buzz, in *Love! Valour! Compassion!* The Off-Broadway part had been played by **Nathan Lane**, whom many claim is America's funniest actor. In the new movie based on **Terrence McNally**'s smash play, the part is played by **Jason Alexander**, a star in the popular "Seinfeld" telecast. In one scene, Alexander appears naked except for an apron, a Panama hat, and red pumps, his endomorphic butt in full view as he bitchily steals one scene after another. "I'm the only straight actor I know of who has played this role," he recently told an *Entertainment Weekly* reporter.

(Jason, Jason, sh! **Nathan Lane** has not yet come out of the closet!)

Another straight actor in *Love! Valour! Compassion!* (no gay actors, it appears, are to be found in Hollywood) is Ramon, a cocky Latino played by **Randy Becker**. Like the rest of the cast of six, he shucks his clothes and cavorts in the nude (to the particular delight of all concerned). With consummate enthusiasm (nay, passion!), he French-kisses one of the weekenders he has just met. And he is entirely credible in an S&M scene in which he is tied to a chair and is abused (with valour!) by his lover of but a few weeks. Most who see the movie will assume Becker is gay, but he is not. And as for whether he was embarrassed at being nude in the movie, Becker ingenuously told a reporter, "It was no big deal." (No, it wasn't, Randy, but it's still above-average.)

.

No gay humanists have come out so far this year. We're still unsure about **Ellen DeGeneres**'s religious makeup (except that she was an atheist at birth), but her April 30th "coming out" show on "Ellen" netted her a Nielsen rating showing 39% of New York City's TV sets were tuned to her station (49% in Boston). In Canada, however, Member of Parliament **Svend Robinson** not only reveals that he is a non-theist but also publicly states that he is gay.

.

HTTP was created for the Internet by a not-gay American humanities humanist, **Ted Nelson** (son of actress **Celeste Holm**). The World Wide Web was created by a British Unitarian, **Tim Berners-Lee**. To the present writer, straight billionaire **Warren Buffet** has confirmed that he is an agnostic.

Meanwhile, Microsoft's straight billionaire, **Bill Gates**, when asked about the supernatural, responded, "I don't know if there's a god or not. Uh, but uh . . . religion principles are quite valid." Perhaps because his wife is Catholic, he quickly added, "Just in terms of allocation of time resources, religion is not very efficient. There's a lot more I could be doing on a Sunday morning."

Winter 1997

In Britain the royal family is having its private *affairs* exposed by *Ms* **Kitty Litter**. Concurrently, in America *Ms* **Paula Jones** is trying to expose our President's privates. Years ago when he was Governor of Arkansas, she says, **Bill Clinton** dropped his trousers and demanded oral sex. Her lips quivering, she has brought charges and demanded that Clinton be photographed to prove her claim that he has "a distinguishing characteristic" known as Peyronie's disease, of which she was witness.

As our parents all taught us, that's when there's a sharp curvature when the penis is erect. Because there is admittedly no direct physical evidence of wrongdoing, poor Paula's perilous predicament is pitiable.

Meanwhile, Bill Clinton's physician has reported that during his annual physical the president was found to be "normal in all respects." (That he is normal, of course, has been known ever since he supported the Armed Forces "Don't ask, don't tell" policy.)

.

The New York Times failed to include in a widely printed photograph taken at **Gianni Versace's** funeral that next to a weeping **Elton John** and **Diana**, the late Princess of Wales, were John's long-time partner, **David Furnish**, as well as Versace's **Antonio D'Amico** (who now will inherit $30,000 per month from the Versace estate).

Gianni Versace's killer, **Andrew Cunanan**, was heavily into sadomasochistic sex, according to **Maureen Orth** in *Vanity Fair* (September '97). He was into drugs, latex, and face masks with just the nostrils showing through. Receipts found in his belongings indicated that he had been in New York City on May 5, 6, 7 and 8. He had seen a movie on 23rd Street near the famed Chelsea Hotel, and he had gone to a west side club that advertises steam rooms, showers, and weights. Muscular types in the gay Greenwich Village and Chelsea areas are wondering if perhaps he may have rubbed up against them.

Nearby, at 206 West 23rd *St*, the "world's first *S&M* cafe" has opened. **La Nouvelle Justine** has waiters with whips, and diners sit in an appropriately depraved environment. Not far away at the 14th Street's **Manhole**, gay as well as straight *S&M* clubs share space. One feature is a motorcycle, upon which a couple may sit and, in between loud slaps, "Thank you, sir" is clearly audible.

Pianist **Van Cliburn**, who won the 1958 Tchaikovsky Competition and went on to accumulate a fortune as a star concert pianist, has won a palimony suit brought by **Thomas Zaremba**. A Texas Court of Appeals dismissed Zaremba's claim that the two had been sexual partners starting in 1966 and that he had provided services "like shopping, doing the mail, paying the bills, drafting checks, co-managing the household, and dealing with accountants, creditors and real estate agents in exchange for a share in Cliburn's income."

In a documentary film about his lifestyle, **Elton John** mentions the fake names he has used when checking in to hotels, such as Sir Colin Chihuahua, Prince Fooboo, and Sir Humphrey Handbag. When his mother once rang up to ask for him when he was registered as Sir Horace Pussy, according to columnist Larry Sutton, the hotel clerk asked "who is calling?" She wasn't too pleased, says Elton, at having to respond, "*Mrs* Pussy."

Challenging an article in *The Advocate* that claimed secular gays and lesbians are indebted to their religious counterparts, **Harley A. Brown** of Philadelphia's gay and lesbian secular humanist group retorted in that magazine (2 September '97) that "It was secular psychologists, anthropologists, sociologists, biologists, and philosophers who developed the humanistic attitudes and scientific basis for the social acceptance of homosexuality. Apart from the Unitarian Universalists, no major straight-controlled churches have been able to immediately accept this because the Bible, 'the word of God,' and irrational faith has stood in the way."

Katha Pollitt, the controversial American writer and secular humanist (for whom religion is "the eternal enemy of human happiness and freedom") has observed that **Princess Diana** and **Mother Teresa** were both "flowers of hierarchical, feudal, essentially masculine institutions in which they had no structural power but whose authoritarian natures they obscured and prettified."

Both, she found, "despite protestations to the contrary, were in the modern mass-market image business. Neither challenged the status quo that produced the social evils they supposedly helped alleviate. In fact, by promoting the illusion that nuns with no medical training, or selling your dresses for charity, could make a difference on a significant scale, they masked those evils or even (in the case of Mother Teresa's opposition to abortion and birth control) made them worse." Why, Pollitt questioned, should children's hospitals require Di's fundraising services instead of receiving adequate support from taxpayers.

Spring 1998

Virgil Thomson, whose *Four Saints in Three Acts* (1928) and *The Mother of Us All* (1947) had operatic librettos by Gertrude Stein, was gay and a non-believer. This is documented in **Anthony Tommasini**'s biography, *Virgil Thomson: Composer on the Aisle* (1997), which includes how the famous composer and influential music critic was once arrested in a male bordello in Brooklyn and how, at the age of ninety, he was wooed by a young admirer. Film buffs know that Thomson's 1949 film score for *Louisiana Story* received the only Pulitzer Prize given for a film. In addition to describing Thomson's distaste for organized religion, the biographer relates how, when in college, Thomson was introduced to and supplied with drugs by a Mormon who had rationalized in a 1918 doctoral dissertation that peyote was not technically a drug, that it allowed one to reach up to the "higher power" and "exalted state" that Jesus Christ had attained. Who was the Mormon? None other than the church founder's grandson, **Dr Frederick Madison Smith**, who himself became the President of the religious group.

In his nineties, Thomson helped pre-plan the final "show" - his own funeral service. He chose it to be held in St John's (Episcopal) Cathedral, which Gothic structure he called "St John the Too-Too Divine." He also chose to die in his sleep, appropriately "in time to make all editions of the Sunday *New York Times*."

Although no speeches or spoken tributes were to be allowed, the cathedral's dean, the **Very Reverend James P Morton**, gave a lengthy, pompous, and inaccurate tribute to Thomson, whom he barely knew, including basic facts of Virgil's life that were incorrect. Later, in the little Missouri cemetery where Thomson's ashes were buried, the local Baptist minister overlooked Virgil's distaste for organized religion, saying, "Virgil's parents were Baptists through and through. Virgil was read to from the Bible. Virgil was raised a Baptist, and that was important." He then read two Psalms of David, a chapter from *Revelation*, and a passage from *John*. Just as plans in life go awry, so in death.

.

Lou Harrison, sometimes dubbed the senior gay composer in the United States, has been honored by issuance of a new compact disc, *Lou Harrison: A Portrait* (Argo, 1997), performed by the California Symphony Orchestra and conducted by **Barry Jekowsky**. The eighty-year-old's work is contained in an eighty-minute anthology that illustrates why his avant-garde 1940s music brought him success and a seat in the American Academy of Arts and Letters. A "cardbearing humanist" and devotee of **Lucretius** and **Epicurus**, Harrison has lived in Aptos, California, since 1967 with **William Colvig**, a contractor and member of an electricians' union.

.

Ned Rorem, sometimes described as music's elder statesman as well as its enfant terrible, is another musician who is an atheist and does not believe in an afterlife. He remains a nominal member of his parents' church, the Society of Friends, because "For better or worse I believe that all war is wrong at all times. But I never go to meeting . . . any more than to Alcoholics Anonymous meetings, the tenets of which I nonetheless observe." Rorem believes that gay-rights groups should seek to abolish the military, not achieve fuller representation in it.

To a *Times* reporter (28 *Jan* 1998), Rorem said, "I don't think life has a purpose. We invent purposes to get through life. I feel basically good, but I am surrounded by death, the deaths of friends, and friends' mates, and every time it is unbearable. I don't believe in God, and I know there is no afterlife. Yet I do believe in belief. I'm not moved by the belief of the Moonies, but I am by the belief of **Michelangelo**, **King David**, and [social critic and pacifist] **Paul Goodman**."

Rorem's *Paris Diary* (1966) shocked many with its revelations about his and others' sexual escapades as, for example, "I can't sleep with famous people. Or for that matter with rich people, or people in power, used to being the center of attention. I have been in bed with four *Time* covers - **Lenny Bernstein**, **Tennessee Williams**, **Noel Coward**, and **John Cheever** (included among 3,000 proportionately anonymous souls, including one woman) - and I performed out of a combination of duress and politeness." For twenty-seven years, Rorem has lived monogamously with **James Holmes**, an organist and choir director.

Summer 1998

It is the best of times. It is the worst of times. It is the gossipiest of times. It has probably always been so. Even the ancients were intrigued by the story of **Adamastor**, whose penis was so monstrously huge that he and the nymph **Thetis** were unable to have sex. Or by the whispered rumor that **Alcibiades**, when not attempting to seduce **Socrates**, went around drunkenly knocking phalluses off public statues.

American universities in large numbers have now instituted "queer studies programs." Their scope was touched upon in a March television show, the popular "60 Minutes" program. In it, one professor related how the 28-year-old lawyer **Abraham Lincoln** had shared a double bed for four years with 23-year-old **Joshua Fry Speed**. That news came as no surprise to those who had already known that President **James Buchanan** (1857-1861), our only bachelor president and once our minister to Great Britain, had been roommates for over two decades with Alabama Senator **William Rufus de Vane King** who reportedly was called "Miss Nancy" by Washingtonians of that day.

Gore Vidal's *Palimpsest* (1995) had details about numbers of world leaders, including several about his fellow promiscuous friend **Jack Kennedy**. When Kennedy was only the President-elect, he is said to have grinned when called "the President-erect." Vidal, the atheist admirer of **Lucretius**, told how **Tennessee Williams**, when visiting, had found Kennedy sexually attractive. "Look at that ass." Tennessee had told Vidal as the three of them were being shown around. "You can't cruise our next president," Vidal told him sternly.

But later when Vidal told Kennedy, Kennedy had grinned and said, "That's very exciting."

Vidal's tales about various VIPs also include one about the **Bishop of Ephesus**. In his *Live From Golgotha* (1982), Vidal described the bishop, the heterosexual Timothy, as having had "the largest dick in our part of Asia Minor." Further, he was represented as having been an acolyte and "love toy" of *St Paul* . . . which should give women adequate ammunition for their feminist canons.

·

This year, numbers of women are eager to obtain advances from publishers for their material about alleged sexual advances by **President Bill Clinton**, who understandably chose to leave for an extended tour of Africa, where he drew bigger crowds than the **Pope**, probably because of his greater sex appeal.

·

At the Oscars, **Dustin Hoffman**, introducing a short clip that featured all sixty-nine Best Picture winners at this year's Oscar Awards, mused whether "the number 69 is as significant internationally as it is at home." Meanwhile, rumors fly about Dustin's demands that all movie shots of him be personally checked to insure that he is not shown to have a limp wrist.

·

Jodie Foster, who has come out as a freethinker, now says she is pregnant. "I couldn't be happier," she told columnist **Liz Smith**, "but, no, I'm not going to discuss the father, the method, or anything of that nature." **Sandra Bernhard** is giving no clue as to the father of her forthcoming baby, except to say she had insisted the donor be Jewish. Upon arrival, of course, the babies will touch down as non-theists - any religious baggage gets checked aboard later.

·

The cognoscenti are presently marveling about two works that describe the sexual appetites of VIPs. *Josephine*, an overlooked 1993 work by **Josephine Baker's** "adopted children" **Jean-Claude Baker** and **Chris Chase**, has juicy gossip about Baker's bisexual escapades with numbers of noted as well as not-so-noted admirers, and tells of her gay fourth husband, **Jo Bouillon**. Jean-Claude, who runs a spiffy restaurant in Manhattan's theatre district, has been seen goosing one of his handsome waiters.

·

Meanwhile, even in Sri Lanka they are talking about a work that tells how a dirt-poor Depression-era American boy becomes an oral delight and sex partner of the rich and beautiful in the international social world. Based on an actual 1943 murder, the novel drops names such as **Maxine Elliott**, said to have been **Edward VII's** mistress; describes the **Duke and Duchess of Windsor**; and includes tales about **Cole Porter**, **Clifton Webb**, **Gloria Swanson**, **Elsa Maxwell**, **Joan Crawford**, **Marlene Dietrich**, **Pablo Picasso**, **Barbara Stanwyck**, **Tallulah Bankhead**, and others.

The author of *The Good Life* (1997) is **Charles G. Hulse**, who completed his lover **Gordon Merrick's** unfinished work. In 1988, Merrick died in Sri Lanka, where Hulse lives part-time and the rest of the time in France.

Autumn 1998

This year's Stonewall Parade was again led by members of the **Stonewall Veterans' Association**. Although hundreds claim to have been on hand in 1969 during the five days of riots, only five of us marched the entire distance from 52nd Street past St. Patrick's to Christopher Street in Greenwich Village: **Stephen van Cline**, **Jeremiah Newton**, **Danny Garvin**, **Sylvia Rey Rivera**, and **Warren Allen Smith**. As the parade of thousands passed the cathedral, many marchers pointed and yelled "Shame!" Sylvia, who marches every year, wrenched her back and had to be carried the last five blocks. All the while she kept yelling to bystanders, "We are your history!" And they lustily cheered back, block after block.

.

HUMANIST LESBIAN HAS BABY! That could have been, but wasn't, the headline when Oscar-winner actor **Jodie Foster**, 35, gave birth to a 7½-pound boy she has named Charles. When she starred in *Contact*, the movie inspired by humanist **Carl Sagan's** 1985 novel, Foster told the press that she had never believed in God nor practiced a religion. In addition to coming out as a freethinker in 1997, she also came out as a lesbian. Because Foster refuses to name the father, wags are betting whether or not the baby - born an atheist, of course - will have two mommies.

.

Journalists flitted crazily as **Hillary and Bill Clinton** flew this past summer to nearby Long Island, where **Steven Spielberg** was their host. Well over $1 million was collected for the Democratic Party at three bashes attended by notables from all over. One bash was hosted by **Jonathan Sheffer**, founder of the Eos orchestra.

Although his $1.6-million converted barn house was featured in all the news stories, no one seemed to notice it is co-owned with Sheffer's companion, *Dr* **Christopher Barley**.

Now that O. J. Simpson is passé, newspapers are increasing their circulation with stories about the President's involvement in a sex scandal (wags say the gal was outfitted with White House knee pads). Readers, however, failed to notice that reporters at the bash wrote that the President was treated to puffer fish rather than to the delicacy's actual name: blowfish.

.

Actor-singer **Bruce Willis**, who is married to **Demi Moore**, recently went on record as saying: "Organized religions in general, in my opinion, are dying forms. They were all very important when we didn't know why the sun moved, why weather changed, why hurricanes occurred, or volcanoes happened. Modern religion is the end trail of modern mythology. But there are people who interpret the Bible literally. *Literally*! I choose not to believe that's the way."

.

Stephen Sondheim, who may be Jewish although others say he is a secularist, has finally acknowledged his homosexuality. **Meryle Secrest**'s *Stephen Sondheim: A Life* (1998) describes his working relationship with **Leonard Bernstein** (who once accepted an American Humanist Association award) and tells of his dating women while having relations with men. In 1991, he said he fell in love for the first time in his life, to **Peter Jones**, a young writer. The book includes a showbiz tale about **Larry Kert**, who was so tired during a 1972 London opening of *Company* that he strode to the front of the stage and said, "Who do I have to screw to get out of this show?" After a moment of silence, Sondheim's voice was heard from the back: "Same person you screwed to get in."

.

An old story still going the rounds in Manhattan: **Sean Connery** on the **Dame Edna Everidge** Show is asked, "Well, Sean, what **James Bond** film was it where your nude body was exposed and on which one saw a crawling spider?" "A spider! On me? Never! That was a stunt man," exclaimed Connery. The guest seated to Connery's left, however, chimed in, "Well, really now, it looked like a spider to me!"

.

"Queer," which has been used disparagingly since the 1920s, is increasingly being adopted as a preferred term by radical homosexuals, particularly in the American academic community. Or so the forthcoming *Random House Webster's Dictionary* will state. Mainstreamers, however, continue to use gay and lesbian as the terms of choice.

Winter 1998

His problem is on everyone's tongue. Not just **Monica Lewinsky's**.

Gay and lesbian humanists at first assumed that "impeachment" referred to **President Bill Clinton's** curious Baptist custom of feeling guilty each time a Jewish girl showed her thong and started things, then of his finishing up solo in the bathroom.

But, no, it turns out to mean that according to the US Constitution if a person is asked under oath about his private sex life, he must - *se offendeno*, as even **Ophelia's** gravediggers knew - be impeached in the event he skirts the issue or jockeys with legalisms.

Lawyers now look forward greedily to querying politicians, not just gay and lesbian members of the armed forces, about their private affairs. Already three Republicans have confessed to having had adulterous affairs, too: House Judiciary Committee Chairman **Henry Hyde** (who presided over Clinton's impeachment inquiry), House Speaker-not-to-be **Bob Livingston** (who favored Clinton's impeachment for lying), and Indiana Representative **Dan Burton** (who, although accused of sleeping with female staff and groping a lobbyist, once called Clinton an immoral "scumbag"). Female Republicans also are confessing: Idaho Representative **Helen Chenoweth** has admitted to having had "it" with a married man, but "I've asked for God's forgiveness, and I've received it."

.

Secrets, alas, used to involve privates. "Faith, her privates we," **Rosencrantz** and **Guildenstern** told **Hamlet** when asked for the truth. These days, however, royalty finds itself being fervently photographed in the nude. Clinton's curved privates are no longer so private. And Massachusetts Representative **Barney Frank's** breakup of a ten-year relationship with **Herb Moses** has been outed. To bring things to a head, one is no longer even certain what is meant by a "member" of Congress.

As America goes, so goes the world. Already the appropriately named **Rev. Canaan Banana**, formerly the President of Zimbabwe, has been caught. He was convicted in November of sodomy with young bodyguards, gardeners, and cook. Also, Malaysia's former Deputy Prime Minister **Anwar Ibrahim** has been in court for allegedly having sodomized his wife's former chauffeur. Nova Scotia's former premier, **Gerald Regan**, was tried but found not guilty of rape, attempted rape, and indecent assault upon three women. So, who next, now that the suspected virgin **Mother Teresa** is no longer alive to preach against the pleasures of sex!

.

Gays and lesbians who are Republicans (conservatives, moderates) have hoped that Clinton will get kicked out. Those who are Democrats (moderates, liberals) have hoped he'll finish out his presidency. Many remain angry that Clinton in his World AIDS Day remarks did not mention gay people, that his administration has opposed needle-exchange programs, that it fired **Joycelyn Elders** as Surgeon General for speaking out about safe sex and condoms, and that it has rendered gays and lesbians second class citizens in the military and in marriage. In the Puritanical environment we inherited from England, Americans generally think that Clinton has betrayed friends and colleagues, has done a good job as President during a period of prosperity, did not deserve **Judge Starr's** (a minion of the tobacco lobby) and the Republicans' mirthless satire of attempting an entrapment and coup d'état, and has given the fine old term "philandering" a dirty name.

.

Quentin Crisp, the gay non-theist, spent Christmas off-Broadway celebrating his 90th birthday. The ex-Britisher who wrote *The Naked Civil Servant* in 1968, tells Yanks that **Lady Diana**, before she was **Princess Diana**, knew that royal marriages are never about love. Didn't **Queen Alexandra**, Crisp relates, when **Edward VII** was on his deathbed and knowing about his mistress, say, "Let **Mrs Kepple** be sent for"? In England, Crisp wittily says in his Gay Nineties show: "Adultery is condoned, divorce is not. In the United States it's the opposite. Every American woman knows marriage is for a little while alimony is forever."

Two leading gay playwrights, both humanists, have had big successes in New York. **Terrence McNally's** *Corpus Christi* was a memorable dramatic experience. Ticket holders started by passing through a group of protesting religious fundamentalists in order to get in, then they passed through a metal detector to make sure that whatever the guard saw bulging wasn't a gun. The play was panned by theists with a vested interest, of course. However, its central theme - acceptance of outsiders and the need for tolerance - was praised by the cognoscenti. Its lead character, a Texan named **Joshua**, spread his Jesus-like gospel of affirmation in saying to his childhood lover, **Judas**, and others, "God loves us most when we love each other." Judas, of course, betrays him to "the fag haters in priests' robes,' and Joshua is crucified by the very ones who jeered him as a young boy, something with which it is easy to empathize. But many found the work less impious than **Monty Python's** *The Life of Brian* or *Jesus Christ Superstar*.

Far more blasphemous is **Paul Rudnick's** *The Most Fabulous Story Ever Told*, one of the theatrical season's funniest comedies. God, according to Rudnick, actually created **Adam** and **Steve** as well as **Janet** and **Mabel**, not just **Adam** and **Eve**. The same-sex couples quickly fall for each other. Adam is unsure where he came from, but he does find Eden a "fabulous" place except - true to his orientation as a nervous aesthete - is concerned about his hair and says, "I mean, I would have put the lake over there." Steve is the secular humanist type who points out that the Bible has to be wrong because, look, there's no Eve. Janet, meanwhile, is the butch type. Mabel's a dippy spiritual sort.

This is a delightfully irreverent work, guaranteed to rile the religious right, particularly because of some frontal nudity (the cute priest, alas, never gets unfrocked) and a scene with godly-possible backdoor intercourse. "Believe in not knowing" and "Take a real risk - ask nothing" are two statements playgoers receive from the script. In Britain, pray that the play will be resurrected there - don't miss any such second coming. Also pray for a resurrection of Rudnick's 1990s play, *The Naked Eye* in which a man on a cross has an erection.

.

The Winter Solstice arrived in Manhattan at 20:56 on December 21 almost entirely unnoticed except by secular humanists who were not taking advantage of the ChristMyth 60% Off sales.

Spring 1999

"It may be that our role on this planet is not to worship God , , , but to create him," **Sir Arthur C. Clarke** mused long ago. The eminent non-believer, who loves to reminisce about his stay in Manhattan's Hotel Chelsea, not only has agreed to being a member of the Dadaistic **National Church of the Exquisite Panic** but also of the philosophy-pursuing **FANNY (Freethinking Activist Non-believing New Yorkers)**. Since 1956 the inventor of the communication satellite (COMSAT) has lived in Sri Lanka and in 1975 was honored as a Resident Guest. "When anyone asks if I'm gay," said Sir Arthur on New Year's Eve in 1997, "I answer, 'No, just slightly cheerful.' "

On February 19th, Sir Arthur was honored by a Sri Lankan stamp that commemorates his adopted island's 50 years of communication. On the double 3.5 rupee stamps, he is pictured twice, once as he looked five decades ago and once as he looks now. He thus becomes the only living secular humanist to be pictured on a postage stamp.

"How do you tell a Maldivian from a Sri Lankan?" I innocently e-mailed a British novelist, not Sir Arthur, who is currently writing about both islands. "Maldivians are circumcised," he responded with a sound bite. "Sri Lankans aren't." His first-hand observations, I am sure, were based on seeing Muslims in the Maldives and Buddhists in Sri Lanka.

"And how do you tell a Yank from a Limey?" he playfully retorted. My research revealed that in the 1960s an estimated 95% of American-born boys were circumcised before they left the hospital. Very few were in England. According to a 1997 University of Chicago study, the practice in the States was most prevalent among white men and men from educated families - 96% in Jewish families questioned, but only 54% for Hispanic men.

The March issue of *Pediatrics* reports that in the American West, with large populations of Hispanic and Asian immigrants, who do not usually circumcise, the rate now is just 36%. Except for Israel, the United States is the only Western country that still circumcises a majority (66% in 1995) of baby boys. But the trend is downward, and the American Academy of Pediatrics has just issued a new finding that there is no "medical indication" for circumcision. As a result, it may become increasingly more difficult, I e-mailed the novelist, to tell a Yank from a Limey.

.

Here in Greenwich Village, the *Village Voice* reports that inflation has set in, that $500 was charged in 1996 "for hacking a foreskin." Jewish comics have long been known to say that although a mohel - the hacker - doesn't get paid much, he does get good tips.

Critics cite *Acts* 15, which states that Christians need not practice circumcision. Meanwhile, some children in presumably frivolous lawsuits have demanded of parents that they replace their lost foreskins.

Humanist leaders, of course, long have said that the practice should be for medical reasons only. In 3001, according to **Sir Arthur C. Clarke**, much will have changed. The eminent secular humanist writes in *3001*, "Circumcision made a lot of sense in primitive times but no longer. By the mid-twenty-first century so many malpractice suits had been filed that the American Medical Association had been forced to ban it. The practice, however, continued a century later, until some unknown genius coined a slogan - please excuse the vulgarity - 'God designed us: circumcision is blasphemy.' "

.

Sylvia Townsend Warner (1893-1978), a strongly anticlerical British novelist who wrote "potboilers" for *The New Yorker* from 1936 on, enjoyed four decades of devotion with **Valentine Ackland**, a gal who had boldly changed her name from Molly, cut her hair in an "Eton crop," and often was mistaken for a good-looking guy. *I'll Stand By You* (1999), a collection of their love letters, is up toward the top of the list of American lesbians' reading. When Ackland converted to Roman Catholicism near the end of her life, Warner had to put up with the sight of rosaries and prayer books around the house.

.

Candace Gingrich, a lesbian and gay rights activist, is a non-theist. **Newt**, her half-brother and a Baptist who was a national Republican leader, has expressed his displeasure with the "life style" his half-sister has "chosen." She has stated, "I would have to be considered an agnostic at best. In my own life, I haven't found a need for organized religion. With all the hostile messages coming at me, including from the emissaries of various faiths, it's more urgent to believe in myself. Ultimately, we all have a responsibility to remind ourselves of our ability to be compassionate, respectful, and generous."

.

Composer and non-theist **Ned Rorem** has lost his companion to cancer. **James Holmes**, 59, a composer, choir director, organist, and Rorem's lover since 1967, died in December.

Spring 2000

If there were a past life (for who would foolishly choose to hope for a future life) and I could *become* anyone of my choosing, I would choose to have been **Sergei Diaghilev** (1872 – 1929) or **Paul Cadmus** (1904 - 1999).

As **Diaghilev** I could have been loved by **Nijinsk**y and revered by such as **Picasso**, **Stravinsky**, and **Cocteau**. But as Cadmus, I could have been loved by photographer **Jared French** and model-musician **Jon Andersson** and revered by such as **W. H. Auden, Christopher Isherwood, George Balanchine, George Platt Lynes, George Tooker, Lincoln Kirstein** (New York City Ballet Director, the husband of Paul's sister Fidelma), and **E. M. Forster** (who, while posing for a portrait, passed the time reading aloud passages from *Maurice*).

As a journalist some years ago at the annual ceremonial of the **American Academy of Arts and Letters**, I commenced a friendship with Cadmus when he inquired and learned that I write for *Free Inquiry* and other humanist publications. Asked by this controversial and eminent painter of *The Fleet's In!* and *The Seven Deadly Sins* what I meant by "humanist," I responded in such a way that he replied, "Oh then, *I'm* a secular humanist also!" From then on, whenever we were together, he jovially introduced us as "two secular humanists."

He told me, however, that he had never been much of a student of philosophy. From my description of "naturalistic humanism," however, he agreed that he fit in to its non-supernaturalistic outlook and its emphasis upon the humanities. Later, we both came to prefer **"humanistic naturalism"** as a label, one that **John Dewey** also had once used and which emphasizes the non-supernaturalism.

A devout Catholic until he was seventeen, Cadmus then "shed it all," he said. 'I've always liked the story of the **Albigensians** who were besieged by the Pope at Beziers. His soldiers asked him: "How do we know the heretics from the Christians?" The Pope replied, "Burn them all. God will know his own." A gentle man who seldom raised his voice against anything or anyone, he laughed almost as softly as he played his beloved grand piano, surrounded by books, sculpture, photographs, and different kinds of art.

At one lunch he prepared for me at his Connecticut home, Cadmus said, "I think my ancestors sailed from Jutland around 1710. My father's side may have been Dutch and, like Erasmus, Latinized the name. My mother, conceived in Spain, was born in New York. Her father was Basque, her mother Cuban. Maybe I was just a cad to begin with," he joked, "and the name was Latinized." His parents, both artists, encouraged their son and their daughter, **Fidelma**, to study art, and Cadmus began with an interest in antiques. One day at the National Academy of Design in uptown Manhattan and knowing that older art students had nude models to work with, he peered through a peephole and saw a naked female. "I had never seen a stranger in the nude. It was a revelation," he confirmed telling others. While growing up in Manhattan, he said, "I was fascinated by the sailors around the Soldiers and Sailors Monument. I was young and was propositioned many times. But I was afraid to go with them, and we just talked while sitting on the benches."

"The male nude has been a specialty of my own oeuvre," Cadmus told several friends, "when I am not being concerned with the foibles of people in daily life: men, women, and children. . . . We are made, we are told, "in God's image," and we assume that He was not clothed by Armani or Brooks Brothers or, if He is She, not attired by Balenciaga or Donna Karan."

Cadmus, who in 94 years completed over 120 paintings, delighted in such observations. "I do love **Michelangelo**'s male forms," he has said, adding that "Michelangelo's women often look like males with grapefruits attached. . . . It seems that genitalia,
Cadmus lamented about the public taste, "equal pornography." But not for him personally: "My penis is not the most important organ in my body. My *eyes* are."

Cadmus met **Jon Andersson**, 27, when he himself was 59 and "I never wanted to be with anyone else." That included the time he was invited to a long-ago party by **Truman Capote**. Capote's long-time companion **Jack Dunphy** told him he could not bring a male guest, that "Truman said he didn't want to ask 'a bunch of fags' to his party." This infuriated Andersson and was one of the few times the two did not appear together in public or private. On one occasion when it was said that he was the only artist to draw so many male nudes, the then 92-year-old Cadmus quipped, "Well, there was Michelangelo."

Biographer **Charles Kaiser** quotes Cadmus as having been interviewed by **Alfred Charles Kinsey**: "He took homosexuality just as calmly as he did his work with wasps. He interviewed me about my sex life – how many orgasms, how big it was, measure it before and after." Kinsey even went to dinner at Cadmus's house following the interview.

Just before his 95th birthday on December 17th, friends were invited on December 1st to a birthday party at Manhattan's D. C. Gallery. Painters **Jack Levine** and **Chuck Close**, sculptor **Phylis Raskind**, photographer **Charles Henri Ford** (once **Tchelitchew**'s lover), and over one hundred other friends were on hand to toast Cadmus and celebrate his birthday. Cadmus walked spryly and greeted everyone joyfully. I was introduced as "a fellow secular humanist," and he and Jon were elated to meet my present companion, a descendant of Maroons who is four decades my junior.

As always, Cadmus gazed with an artist's eye. Eleven days later, and just five days before his actual birthday, Cadmus died peacefully while watching television with Jon at their suburban home in Connecticut.

Summer 1999

Ian McKellen is the Tony Award-winning actor who continually receives favorable publicity in all the American gay journals. "Is he married?" some potential suitors ask. "Hardly." they are informed. "In fact, in England he's a Knight Bachelor!"

Although Sir Ian seldom is quoted for the revelation, he told **Tim Appelo** of *Mr Showbiz* (19 January 1996), "I was brought up a Christian, low church, and I liked the community of churchgoing. That's rather been replaced for me by the community of people I work with. I like a sense of family, of people working together. But I'm an atheist. So God, if She exists, isn't really a part of my life."

.

Barry Manilow was recently asked if he believed in God and said, "Yes. His name is **Clive Davis**, and he's the head of my record company." Asked then about how important his Judaism is, he responded, "It isn't. My humanism is."

.

At **Rubyfruit**, a prime lesbian bar and Manhattan restaurant, gals were gossiping recently about **Pamela Anderson**'s having her famous breast implants surgically removed. They were too big, she complained, and she didn't need all that attention. A quick call to a local surgeon turned up the fact that not one male, to his knowledge, has yet signed up for analogous penile surgery.

.

New York City's mayor, **Rudy Giuliani**, has become known as the leader who turned our 1950s to 1990s Fun City into our 1990s Glum City. All gay movies, public toilets and bath houses are now strictly supervised, cinema ushers armed with flashlights lighting up the dark corners of various establishments. However, London gay humanists **Derek Lennard** and **Malcolm Barnes** recently took in the Times Square, Chelsea, and Greenwich Village areas, paid tribute to **Gertrude Stein**'s statue, and ended up getting high. On a helicopter trip over Manhattan and being eye-to-eye with the Statue of Liberty, that is.

.

In some of the more crowded Greenwich Village and Chelsea bars, "fly fishing" has taken on an entirely new meaning.

.

Quentin Crisp, the 90-year-old ex-British author of *The Naked Civil Servant*, continues to receive attention for his viewpoints. Regarding **Monica Lewinsky**, he commented, "In the reign of **Queen Elizabeth I**, if any commoners told tales about sexual encounters with the head of state, they were beheaded." Asked by a young man if he should tell his mother he's gay, Crisp retorted, "Don't tell your mother *anything*!"

.

Religion is being satirized in *Onion*, a Shamanistic Midwestern publication that is online.

Recent stories have had these headlines: DRUGS WIN DRUG WAR, about public-policy shorfalls; FROG WITH HUMAN HEAD WARNS DANGERS OF GENETIC ENGINEERING, about the era of scientific wonders; and ANIMAL RIGHTS ACTIVISTS RELEASE 71,000 COWS INTO WILD, about environmental activists.

In one story, which appears to be a heartwarming account of a little paralyzed boy who prays for recovery, the headline is NO, SAYS GOD.

Another story in its entirety:

> Vanimo, Papua New Guinea - In His first official statement since the July 17 tsunami that claimed the lives of an estimated 3,000 Papua New Guineans, The Lord announced Monday that He killed the island villagers as part of His longtime "moving in mysterious ways" policy, calling the natural disaster "part of My unknowable, divine plan for mankind."

Humor, so it goes, may be the best weapon!

Autumn 1999

Royston Ellis
England's Teenage Allen Ginsberg

Whatever happened to the teenage beatnik poet often described as England's Allen Ginsberg? The answer is that he's alive and well, has been traveling all around the world since he left England at the age of twenty, and today he is somewhere in Southeast Asia.

Royston Ellis left school at the age of sixteen and as a teenager toured with the Beatles when they were starting out as the Beetles. He convinced them they were part of the Beats, individuals unfairly being beaten down simply because they were unconventional, and they agreed to the change in spelling. While they provided the music at events, Ellis provided the rocketry (poetry read to rock 'n' roll). Also, he showed **John Lennon** and **Paul McCartney** how to break down a Benzedrine nose inhaler and sniff the strips inside in order to produce a mild high. This was, Lennon later recounted, their first experience with drugs.

Steve Turner, in *Cliff Richard, The Biography* (1993), describes Ellis as

> . . . Britain's first teenage pundit, an Allen Ginsberg of suburban London. The fact that he wore a beard and had worked as an office boy, duster salesman, gardener, milk-bottle washer, building

labourer, and farm hand by the age of eighteen helped confirm the image. . . . His first volume of poems, *Jiving to Gyp*, was dedicated [to **Cliff Richard**], and he was soon asked by television programmes to explain what teenagers were all about. He ended up with his own series, "Living For Kicks," in which he explored the controversial issues of the day such as pep pills and sex before marriage.

"One in every four men is homosexual," Ellis told McCartney, according to Barry Miles's *Paul McCartney* (1998):

So we looked at the group! One in every four! It literally meant one of us is gay. Oh, fucking hell, it's not me, is it? We had a lot of soul-searching to do over that little one.

The "one" was their manager, **Brian Epstein**, who in 1962 signed a management contract with them for twenty-five per cent of their gross receipts, after a certain threshold was reached and after he got them a recording contract.

Ellis, a cogent musical commentator - his 1961 paperback *The Big Beat Scene* still stands up as an appraisal of early British rock 'n' roll - had met the fledgling Beatles in May 1960. "The first time we ever heard about gayness was when a poet named Royston Ellis arrived in Liverpool with his book *Jiving With Gyp*," McCartney has recalled. "He was a Beat poet. Well, well! Phew! You didn't meet them in Liverpool. And it was all 'Break me in easy, break me in easy . . . .' It was all shagging sailors, I think. We had a laugh with that line."

McCartney's biographer adds the following concerning Ellis's close friendship with the Beatles:

'Polythene Pam' was another of John's songs written in India and originally destined for the White Album. It was inspired by Stephanie, a girlfriend of the Beat poet Royston Ellis, whom the Beatles backed at Liverpool University in 1960. On 8 August 1963, the Beatles played at the Auditorium in Guernsey, the Channel Islands. Royston Ellis was working as a ferryboat engineer on the island and invited John to come back to his flat. John told *Playboy*: 'I had a girl and he had one he wanted me to meet. He said she dressed up in polythene, which she did. She didn't wear jackboots and kilts, I just sort of elaborated. Perverted sex in a polythene bag.

Just looking for something to write about.' Royston Ellis told Steve Turner: 'We all dressed up in them and wore them in bed. John stayed the night with us in the same bed.' Paul remembered meeting Royston in Guernsey: 'John, being Royston's friend, went out to dinner with him and got pissed and stuff and they ended up back at his apartment with a girl who dressed herself in polythene for John's amusements, so it was a little kinky scene. She became Polythene Pam. She was a real character.' John: 'When I recorded it I used a thick Liverpool accent because it was supposed to be about a mythical Liverpool scrubber dressed up in her jackboots and kilt.'

I first met Ellis when my syndicated column, "Manhattan Scene" in West Indian islands, appeared in *The Educator*, which he was editing in Dominica and where he was the Reuters correspondent. At that time he was a real estate developer for the Marquis of Bristol, and we learned that we shared in common a liking for champagne and caviar. "Partial to black seeds," we found.

Under the pseudonym **Richard Tresillian**, he became a best-selling author of The Bondmaster series - over a million copies of the paperbacks with a historical background were sold and described the lives and loves of 19th century West Indian whites and the workers on their estates. Under the same pseudonym he wrote a best-selling series, Fleshtraders, again about 19th century miscegenation and adventures but this time set in Mauritius.

Since he moved to Sri Lanka in 1981, he has become a travel author, a lecturer on the *Queen Elizabeth 2's* trip between Bombay and Singapore, and an author on various topics.

In 1983, some of his poetry was included in *The Penguin Book of Homosexual Verse*, poems from his "Cherry Boy." He has written extensively about railroads in Sri Lanka and is known for his definitive guide to the 7,000 railroads in India and for his travel guidebook about Mauritius. His most recent work, *A Man for All Islands* (1998), is a biography of **Maumoon Abdul Gayoom**, President of the Maldives. With photographer **Gemunu Amarasinghe**, he wrote *A Maldives Celebration*.

In our discussions about philosophy and humanism, Ellis has told me that since the age of fourteen he had decided it was not God who created man but that man had created God. "My first book, *Jiving to Gyp* (gyp means hell), was published when I was 18," he said, "and it contained raunchy atheistic poems." He is nostalgic about having had backing from **The Beatles** and **Led Zeppelin**, and he only returns to England occasionally, loving the adventurous life in the tropics.

Today the Life Fellow of the Royal Commonwealth Society might be on the *QE2*, or seeing one of the Buddha's two known teeth, the one at Kandy in Sri Lanka, or doing a photo-shoot somewhere in Southeast Asia, or just working on a novel that has a Maldivian setting. "How do you tell a Muslim male Maldivian from a Buddhist male Sri Lankan," I recently asked, ingenuously. Lifting his champagne glass, Royston had a quick response: "Remove their clothes."

Royston Ellis: gay secular humanist, writer extraordinaire, lecturer, and modest storyteller.

Autumn 2000

Björk, a recording artist, has gone on record as saying, "If I get into trouble, there's no God or Allah to sort me out. I have to do it myself."

She added, "I do not believe in religion, but, if I had to choose one, it would be Buddhism. It seems more livable, closer to men. I've been reading about reincarnation, and the Buddhists say we come back as animals and they refer to them as lesser beings. Well, animals aren't lesser beings, they're just like us. So I say fuck the Buddhists."

.

Björk is but one of the contemporary musicians whom I list as non-believers in my just-published *Who's Who in Hell: A Handbook and International Directory for Humanists, Freethinkers, Naturalists, Rationalists, and Non-Theists* (NY: Barricade Books, $125 - reviewed in this issue of *G&LH*).

There are other musicians, and the book documents why they are included as non-believers: the composer-conductor **Pierre Boulez**; Scottish pop-rock singer **Justin Currie**; noted composer **David Diamond**; Brazilian musician-songwriter **Gilberto Gil**; composer **Lou Harrison**; popular musician **Billy Joel**; songwriter-entertainer **Tom Lehrer**; singer-entertainer **Barry**

Manilow; violinist **Yehudi Menuhin**, a member of the British Humanist Association; singer-songwriter **Randy Newman**; orchestra conductor **Seiji Ozawa**; French flutist **Jean-Pierre Rampal**; the **Residents**, a San Francisco-based band; composer **Ned Rorem** (see *CD* review, this issue); folksinger-composer **Pete Seeger**; recording artist **Al Stewart Anthony Tommasin**'s ; and vocalist **Michael Stipe**.

CNN did a story about the book, filming me and my current 32-year-old companion. When National Public Radio interviewed me, the subjects of atheism, gays, and lesbians were freely discussed. In the numerous other radio interviews, I did not hesitate to mention my being gay and a Humanist, and to my pleasant surprise no negative flak has yet ensued. However, a Brazilian journalist complained that I'd omitted their **President Fernando Cardoso**.

Also, I've learned that Chile's President **Ricardo Lagos** is a socialist agnostic. Since the book was published, **Jane Fonda** not only left her freethinking husband **Ted Turner** (who once described Christianity as "a religion for losers") but also gave up her own freethinking and became a Born-Again. As the secular Humanist **Kurt Vonnegut Jr.** would say, "So it goes!" For details about the above monumental book, which lists this magazine and has page after page about humanism and gay topics, go to http://humanists.net/wasm/rationalistsny.htm

.

First, the celebrities **Ellen DeGeneres** and **Anne Heche** broke up. Now the rock star **Melissa Etheridge** and director **Julie Cypher** have broken up, reportedly vowing to remain friends for the sake of their young children.

One celebrity who will never need to divorce is the non-believer **Jodie Foster**. She simply never got married and has never revealed who sired her child.

Winter 2000

Quentin Crisp died one year ago last November. To commemorate his death, a gathering of photos and paintings about his life was shown at a gallery on the Lower East Side.

When he spoke once at a Universalist Society meeting in Manhattan, the British-born author of *The Naked Civil Servant* who fled decades ago to New York City told me he was not a believer in any of the organized religions and also didn't believe in immortality, except in the sense of a creative person's being remembered after his lifetime. Gallery owners knew that Crisp would come to openings if food and drink were available, and in fact he would go anywhere where there were free refreshments.

In 1993 Crisp played the role of **Queen Elizabeth I** in a **Sally Potter** movie, *Orlando*, and he loved Hollywood films. When he reviewed *The Godfather* for a Greenwich Village paper, he noted that the narrative managed to drag in **Pope John Paul I**, who, in real life, Crisp wrote, "died so suspiciously soon after his enthronement [that he was] rumored to have been poisoned with lethal cups of tea." His comments, of course, teed off the Vatican.

At one movie, I sat next to him and inquired if, at the American Embassy in Grosvenor Square, he was once asked if he was a practicing homosexual and had responded, "I didn't practice: I was already perfect." With a touch of the dainty scarf around his neck, Quentin laughed and confirmed the story.

We who attended the November showing of photos and paintings missed seeing Quentin seated somewhere in the gallery. Then again, there were no refreshments!

·

Paul Bowles is back. He arrived at Gate 2 in the *US* Airways terminal at La Guardia at the end of 1999, waiting for a twin-prop commuter plane to fly him to a small town in upstate New York, Glenora.

As described by **Robert Sullivan** in the *New Yorker*, the executor of Bowles's estate, **Joe McPhillips**, headmaster of the American School of Tangier, carried the canister with the Bowles ashes. He had thought Bowles would want to be buried in Tangier but, no, he chose to be buried in the family plot in the vicinity of Lakemont, several miles north of Glenora.

The cemetery overseer had dug a small eighteen-inch-by-eighteen-inch hole for Bowles, and some of those who had heard about the burial appeared and asked if they could touch the canister. "Uh, yes, OK," McPhillips said. Then he showed another box, one he had brought from Tangier, some earth from Morocco and a tape of his music. A coin and some flowers went into the box, the overseer produced a big black plastic bucket full of dirt, and anyone who wanted could help shovel. "I wish we had known you, Paul," said one. Others made personal remarks. No formalities whatsoever for the avowed non-believer!

McPhillips then returned to his car, later concerned that he had forgotten to do something. He had been going to read a scene from Bowles's first novel, *The Sheltering Sky* (1949), in which Port dies. "Oh, dear," he said, aware that it was too late.

Spring 2001

Talk about dishing the dirt! **Christopher Wilson**'s *Dancing with the Devil, The Windsors and Jimmy Donahue* (HarperCollins, £12.50) is in a class with **Jean-Claude Baker**'s *The Josephine Baker Story* and **Gore Vidal**'s *Palimpsest*. It's more mouth-watering than Monicagate!

Wilson's blow-by-blow account tells of the **Duchess of Windsor**'s relations with the **Duke** as well as with **Donahue**, the handsome young grandson of the super-rich "dime store" **Woolworth** family.

Little wonder that Buckingham Palace at the time disliked the Duchess, American-born **Wallis Simpson**. The wonder was that in the 1950s the Duke continued to adore her once it became known that she was romantically involved with Donahue, the colorful and promiscuous homosexual son of a manic depressive and bisexual father. In short: a dysfunctional trio that was bankrolled by Donahue's mother, who delighted in throwing spectacular parties at which the Duke and Duchess became freeloaders.

The book's index is like a who's who of high-society types, many of whom most readers will probably not know were gay.

Oh, the tales Wilson tattles: Oxford students, talking about Hansel and Gretel, romantically linked tutor **Henry Peter Hansel** with his student, **Prince Edward**. After the 1936 abdication, the Duke and Duchess were often strapped for funds. Donahue's mother, despite her huge gambling losses, willingly paid many of their bills, putting them up in the States and displaying them like trophies at her parties. The Duchess, allegedly playing dominatrix, allowed the Duke to dress in diapers while she played Mommy. After years of unfulfilling sex with the Duke, she fell in love with the flamboyantly homosexual Donahue, when he wasn't cruising bars and picking up chorus lads.

Donahue was a school dropout who enjoyed playing expensive practical jokes, including angering an admiral by buzzing his aircraft carrier; dressing as a nun and, squatting in public to defecate, causing gawkers to create a traffic accident; getting thrown out of Italy for standing on a hotel balcony in imitation of **Mussolini**, urinating on the people below; rigging up a microphone when the Windsors visited in order to record the sound of the "royal wee"; shocking some dinner guests by placing his penis on his plate to make it look "like some pink sausage" among the vegetables. The wealthy, spoiled boy's pranks continue on and on.

Donahue was an intimate friend of **Francis Spellman**, New York's gay Cardinal Archbishop, and he mischievously talked the Duke into attending a Christmas Mass at St Patrick's Cathedral, resulting in what "may have been the first British monarch, or ex-monarch, to take the sacrament from a disciple of Rome since the reign of Charles I three hundred years before."

The book's Christian theists all come off looking like hypocrites, of course. But a non-theist - **Ned Rorem**, the nominal Friend who is a pacifist, not a Trinitarian - is inspiringly described as having been hit on by Donahue simply because of his good looks, not because of his musicianship. Rorem was disgusted.

Wilson's book's a hoot, even on this side of the pond!

Summer 2001

At the annual conference of the **Bertrand Russell Society** held in May at Canada's **McMaster University** in Hamilton, Ontario, an award was given to **Stephen Toulmin**, the London-born humanities educator who teaches philosophy at the University of Southern California in Los Angeles. It is a little-known fact that Lord Russell's books, desk, spectacles and writing utensils are among the features of the Russell Archives at McMaster, which draws research specialists from around the world.

This year's discussions critiqued Southampton U's **Roy Monk**, whose loathing of Lord Russell in a new second volume of a two-volume biography, *Bertrand Russell: The Ghost of Madness*, was attacked. Monk stacks the cards against Russell in favor of Russell's gay one-time student, **Ludwig Wittgenstein** (whose cruising in Vienna for rough young men was well known in the first half of the past century). Sir Bertrand the outspoken non-theist was generally backed by American reviewers, who complained that Monk as a biographer did not write a balanced assessment of Russell.

·

Caleb Crain's *American Sympathy: Men, Friendship, and Literature* describes how openly homophobic American society has been in the past but reveals how cleverly, nevertheless, love between men was written about.

Non-theists or borderline non-theists who were mentioned include **Ralph Waldo Emerson** (the Unitarian who translated homoerotic poems of the fourteenth-century Persian poet **Hafiz** and who had a youthful crush on a fellow student named **Martin Gay**); **Henry David Thoreau** (whose journals never mention women and some of whose essays express the beauty and agony of love between men); and **Herman Melville** (author of *Billy Budd*, who recognized that male sexual desires are a fact of shipboard life and who had an unusual emotional attachment to Hawthorne).

Orla Brady, a Dublin-bred author who was raised a Catholic but who now considers herself an atheist, has written a powerful movie, *A Love Divided*, that praises a woman's indomitable spirit against organized religion.

Brady stars in the movie, which tells about a Protestant who marries a Catholic (**Liam Cunningham**). When she chooses not to send their children to a Catholic school despite papers they signed upon being married, she is confronted by a Torquemada-like priest (**Tony Doyle**) who insists that the couple must raise the children as Catholics despite the couple's companion contract to decide all such matters without any outside interference.

Unable to resolve the problem with her husband and fearing she will lose her children, she flees with them from Fethard-on-Sea to friendly Protestants in Scotland. The bigoted Catholic priest in the little coastal town demands that the children return or the Catholic majority will boycott Protestant businesses, friends turn against friends, and the violence that results affects even the town's pub owner, a kindly atheist who is depicted as the only sensible person in town. The surprise ending makes the heterosexual couple's story a metaphor for the larger troubles between the two major theistic groups.

Reportedly, the movie received mixed views in Ireland. In Manhattan, Brady told one reporter that she does not particularly aspire to perfection, that for her very first love scene in a BBC film, "I knew we'd be doing it naked. So I immediately joined a gym, went for two sessions, and bored myself stupid. Real is better - and sexier. Why not just go with that?" (Sure, why not, and thanks for outing yourself as an atheist!)

.

Breaking yet another taboo, one off-Broadway play depicts a father who is estranged from his son but in one scene sodomizes him. The rape, in *Under the Speed of Dreams*, is symbolic as well as mysterious in Chilean **Martin Balmaceda**'s one-act play. A handsome Mexican-American, **Miguel Rivera**, plays the probably homosexual son. In one scene, the father affectionately kisses his son in this magic realist work about love. It is only in the final minutes that theatergoers learn that the son had died, that the action was a depiction of a grieving father who dreamed of earlier and happy days with his wife and son, who lamented that he had not been close to his son, and who now has become a hopeless souse.

.

"Wanna eat my banana?" asked the New York humanist **Doug Fishbone** to surprised Costa Ricans and Poles. Fishbone, a sculptor, arranged for a truckload of bananas to be shipped to the countries' museums, created a banana sculpture, and at the end of the brief show found that museumgoers were happy to take him up on his offer.

Gay friends in Greenwich Village, however, have cautioned him against seeking other places to exhibit, for, inquiring how to extend his project, he has been ingenuously asking experts in the art world, "Show me how to go round the world with this!"

Autumn 2001

This year's **Heritage of Pride Parade** down New York City's Fifth Avenue and on through Greenwich Village was cheered on by several hundred thousand. Again, it featured Stonewall Action Identity League, actual veterans of the 1969 riots, whose president and treasurer are non-theists, as are many of its members. Friends anywhere can join up by going online at

http://humanists.net/wasm/sail.html

.

Could **Chaucer** have been mistaken when he wrote, "This world nys but a thurghfre ful of wo"? The mayor of Paris, **Bertrand Delanoë**, and the acting mayor of Berlin, **Klaus Wowereit**, are not known to be non-believers, but both are gay and not in the closet - not that politicians anywhere want their private lives made public. However, at least admitting one's sexual orientation in today's world is not the same thoroughfare of woe it has been since Chaucer's (and **Oscar Wilde**'s) days.

So what about the mayor of New York City? Well, **Rudy Giuliani** is 101 per cent Catholic (proven by his ability to get a Papal dispensation after having married his first cousin) and such a prude that he "cleaned up" the city's gay spots, forcing many - not just the baths - to go out of business. Imagine the shock, then, that his fellow Catholics have endured upon learning that their devout Rudy has fallen in love with a person not his second wife, the mother of his two children, and that his wife then kicked him out of the city-owned mansion where mayors and their families are supposed to live and, like the British royal family, be models of Christian respectability.

.

So what do you do in a city where even **Monica Lewinsky** is paying $4,000 a month just to rent a little place? Giuliani's solution: save money for the upcoming divorce by bunking in an East Side 32nd-floor flat with his car-dealer friend, **Howard Koeppel**, and Howard's companion, **Mark Hsiao**, and **Bonnie**, the couple's shih tzu. With a gay couple? Yes, begorra, here at the start of **Archbishop Egan**'s new post, which commenced with the summer's gay parade down Fifth Avenue during which he does not dare show his face because marchers pass St Pat's Cathedral, pointing and exclaiming, "Shame, shame!" Just one more problem for the archbishop, along with all those paedophilia cases.

So what do the mayor and the gay couple talk about in the 3,000-square-foot love nest? "I taught him a lot of expressionism." Howard told *New York Times* reporter **Frank Rich**. "He didn't know what a Friend of Dorothy was." Added Mark, "I told him I met **Vladimir Horowitz** in a gay bar." When Howard complained to Rudy about Mark's fetish for pillows, showing him the twenty pillows on their bed, the mayor advised him to cool it: "You can't get upset about things like that. You have trouble with pillows - just imagine what *I'm* going through each day. You're so lucky to have someone like Mark," he added. In a touching gesture, he walked arm-in-arm with Howard in June during part of the gay parade.

Howard, who doesn't dare compare his and Mark's solid partnership with the rancorous disintegration of the mayor's marriage, said he'd like him to stay with them forever, is never bored by but often disagrees with him, and "Actually, I love him. It's not sexual. It's just mental. I have my preferences, and I don't find him attractive at all." Neither does a majority of the gay population, which looks forward to elections in 2002.

.

Non-believing queers have recently allowed the breeders to monopolize the scandal sheets (cabinet meetings in the White House open with **President Select Bush** and his cabinet bowing their Christian heads; Scientologists **Tom Cruise** and **Nicole Kidman** splitting; suicide bombers blowing up people in God's Favorite Battlefield, the Middle East; a 71-year-old Zambian archbishop marrying and possibly impregnating a 43-year-old Korean before being scolded by the Pope; **Prince William**'s allegedly bed-hopping "with a blonde and brunette" on the charity project trip to Chile).

.

It's not known if **Nathan Lane** is a non-believer, but we *are* certain that he's gay, is the funniest actor to hit Broadway in decades and deserves all the attention he is receiving! As Max Bialystock in **Mel Brooks**'s smash hit *The Producers*, Lane wows 'em! Tickets for the outrageously appealing play are the hottest items in town (some being hawked for $1,000 on the Net!). Brooks spares no-one with his satire, which mocks Jews, blacks, Irishmen, old people, gays, lesbians, dumb blondes, even theater people. The plot is the ultimate of tastelessness.

Unlike the **Zero Mostel/Gene Wilder** 1968 film, which was a critical failure but still won an Academy Award, the play is not as harsh or crude but it's gayer, even including a hummable song, "Keep It Gay." In Lane's and **Matthew Broderick**'s search for a moneymaker - the worst play possible, one sure to flop so they can profit by taking the angels' money - they choose *Springtime for Hitler*, by a pigeon-keeping Nazi called Franz Liebkind (**Brad Oscar**) and directed by the ultimate theater queen, Roger De Bris (**Gary Beach**). What a bevy of beauties De Bris has working for (possibly under) him! And **Hitler** comes off as a gay egotist, complete with a middle name of Elizabeth (uh, there's another queen in his lineage).

With a successful flop, the duo look forward to producing other works: *Maim*, *Katz*, *She Shtupps to Conquer*, *Death of a Salesman on Ice*. Mel Brooks's humor is more sophomoric than that of all Harvard, Yale and Columbia sophomores combined. Odds are that, if he could ever be found in a serious mood, he might admit to being a secular or an atheistic Jew. Or simply a laughing humanist!

[This article was written and went to press before the devastating attack committed on New York City on 11 September 2001.]

Winter 2001

When Hell Came to Manhattan

Anyone who has been to my apartment knows that my panoramic view includes the World Trade towers - they're perhaps a little over a mile away, and there are no buildings in between to obstruct my view. I wake up looking at the towers, I look at them all day while at my computer, and when I lie down to go to sleep I look at the beautiful lights, which stay on all night and for that matter all day, too.

When my neighbor telephoned around 09:00 yelling for me to look out my window, I'd gone back to sleep, having gotten up as usual at 04:30 to work on my book, *Celebrities in Hell*, then taken a nap at 08:30. She exclaimed that she didn't understand how I could not have heard the explosion. I had, however, heard a plane fly low and directly over my apartment building - doesn't he know it's illegal to fly over residential areas? I thought to myself! (Only later did I learn that **Mohammed Atta**'s co-pilot had been Allah himself.) I looked out my window, and the north tower had indeed been hit 10 or 20 floors from the top, smoke billowing out. I rang bells on my floor to invite those who don't have my view, then returned with one neighbor and together we watched a plane which I presumed was taking photos of the conflagration. But, no, it zoomed right into the south tower, and flames shot out, this time more toward the bottom of the skyscraper. My feeling? This couldn't be a movie, could it?

I telephoned **Peter Ross**, my computer genius who lives nearby, and was going to stop by anyway to put more memory into my G-4, and he joined me just in time to see the smoke from the two towers billowing over all of the Wall Street area. Something appeared to be falling from windows of the north tower - I'm afraid what I saw were people jumping!

As we watched, yet another hit! The *TV* was blaring, and before long it was speculated that a third plane had hit. However, we could clearly see that, no, no third plane was there. It was an implosion. The building had simply collapsed. Smoke now really increased, and one could imagine people on the ground unable to see where they were going. Then, it appeared despite all the smoke that the building may have buckled. Surely enough, little by little, it was possible to see only the one building standing! Then, and no words can explain the feelings, no, no, no, now the north tower also was falling. Now stupendous smoke! In all likelihood any of the thousands who may have been able to get downstairs in the buildings were down below, looking up at what had happened. And then with all the rescue equipment and people there, both buildings down! And they must have been trapped and covered over, too!

Meanwhile, the telecasts talked about a hit on the Pentagon and other problems. But all I could think of was the loss of life on those hijacked airplanes plus the thousands who were just starting work in the towers and were gone in a second! St Vincent's Hospital is two blocks away, and the ambulance sirens increased even more than usual!

One assumes the terrorists were Muslim. It's clear where this will lead. In short, there's just no place that's safe for a non-believer like me!

It's now over 2 hours later. I look out as I type and I see nothing but a huge, huge cloud of smoke. Presumably the massive towers fell into a huge pile of rubble, bodies and everything in a pile! No television picture can really capture what I'm seeing.

An occasional plane now flies over, and my mind goes back to the war when in Reims we were able to detect the difference in sound of a Nazi or an American plane. Sorry to say, in those days the French came out to look if they heard a Nazi plane but they ran for the shelters if it was an American plane - we dropped a dozen bombs which landed helter-skelter, whereas the Nazis focused carefully, or so the opinions ran at that time.

At any rate, I'm safe. I have electricity. And I have drinking water. Until terrorists take that path, too!

Spring 2002

Sinclair Lewis, who in 1930 became America's first Nobel Prize winner in literature, was a satirist of small-town life in *Main Street*, materialism in *Babbitt*, physicians in *Arrowsmith*, and the clergy in *Elmer Gantry*. Since his time, American freethinkers have never had the same kind of appealing spokesperson, nor have they fully appreciated his importance. Instead, their more noted leaders have focused on their own interest in academic philosophy, partly to cover up their inadequate knowledge of the humanities.

Sinclair Lewis: Rebel from Main Street, a new biography by **Richard Lingeman**, includes the following: "When a writer and editor named **Warren Allen Smith** sent him a questionnaire [in 1950] asking him to choose from several definitions of *humanism* the one most congenial to him, Lewis selected 'naturalistic (scientific) humanism.' To an earlier query about his religion, he contended that people raised without religious belief seemed as happy and as ethical as those who did have a faith." Lewis was said to have been privately homophobic, turned off in London, for example, when he met **Hugh Walpole** and **Lytton Strachey**. Why he described lesbians and their "involuted love" in *Ann Vickers* is of interest, for from 1928 to 1942 Lewis was married to **Dorothy Thompson** and her affection for **Christa Winsloe** was, according to Lingeman, "erotic as well as emotional."

AIDS ACTIVIST **LARRY KRAMER** DIES was the *AP*'s headline in a December 2001 story. However, news of Larry Kramer's death was somewhat exaggerated, for he recovered from a twelve-hour liver-transplant operation on December 21. Kramer, a founder of ACT UP and the author of *The Normal Heart* (1985) and Faggots (1987), was recipient of the 1996 award in literature of the American Academy of Arts and Letters for the screenplay of **D H Lawrence**'s *Women in Love* (1969).

Discussing the notion of evil with the gay journalist and Catholic **Andrew Sullivan** in 1995, Kramer said, "I don't believe in God, so we have to leave him out of it. But I didn't think that the world was evil until the last few years. I've been unwilling to even think of that notion of evil. But I now think that the fact that this plague has been allowed to go on, that so many people have been allowed to die, is just *evil*."

To Sullivan, who like Kramer is HIV-positive, he added that the government could do much more for people with AIDS but "we're now on the third asshole in a row in the White House who simply doesn't want to do anything about it." Kramer's long-time partner, **Rodger McFarlane**, might note that in 2002 Larry, now 66, could change the lament to "the fourth asshole in a row."

·

A few hours before the end of **Rudy Giuliani**'s end of term as puritanical Mayor of New York City, two bars (the Cock and the Hole) celebrated with "backroom" parties (one called Black Sperm Night) that drew dozens of celebrants despite next to no publicity.

Commenting upon the fact that Giuliani was named *Time*'s Man of the Year, the gay non-theist and journalist **Michael Musto** observed, "So were Hitler and Stalin."

·

As to whether three monotheists in the news have gay connections - **John Walker Lindh**, the American who was captured with the Taliban in Afghanistan; **Muhammad Atta**, who piloted the plane that smashed into Tower One of the World Trade Center; and **Adolf Hitler**, who is back in the news because of a new book by **Lothar Machtan**, *The Hidden Hitler* - the gay media have been somewhat reserved.

Lindh's father separated from his wife and moved in with a male companion while John was growing up; and Atta, according to the Mideast expert **Jamie Glazow** of *FrontPage*, has written about Atta's being one of the sexually repressed Arabs in a culture where men's sodomizing of boys is seen as a social norm.

·

Machtan's *The Hidden Hitler* stubbornly amasses trivial facts about Hitler's alleged homosexuality, although documentation is admittedly next to impossible concerning der Führer, the theist whose *Mein Kampf* states: "I am convinced that I am acting as the agent of our Creator. By fighting off the Jews, I am doing the Lord's work."

.

Of more interest to the gay press has been **Mark Bingham**, the handsome gay rugby player who lost his life by foiling the hijackers of United Flight 93, causing it on September 11 to plough into the ground rather than into any buildings in the national capital or elsewhere.

.

Not generally publicized was **Muhammad Atta**'s will with eighteen stipulations, as reported by ABC News. He directed that no-one kiss his dead body; that no pregnant woman or unclean person should approach his body; that he did not want an unnecessary number of people to wash his body; that whoever washed him must wear gloves "so he won't touch my genitals"; that women not go to his grave whatsoever; that he should lie on his right side; and that people who attend his funeral should sit at his grave for an hour "so that I will enjoy their company and slaughter animals and give the meat to the needy." Now that he presumably is in Paradise, one wonders if his reward of 72 vestal virgins will be prohibited from touching him for eternity.

.

Paul Rudnick's *Rude Entertainment* has received mixed reviews but had its audiences howling with laughter. The trio of one-act plays included one about a gay couple hoping to adopt a little girl who says she is from Slomakia, a country torn between the feuding "Turds" and "the Curtsies." The diabolically non-theistic playwright was described in *The Times* as "politically incorrect and proud to show it."

.

Bruce Villanch and other gay movie critics have strongly complained that the script of *A Beautiful Mind*, in which **Russell Crowe** plays the Princeton mathematician **John Nash**, fails to reveal that Nash was known to be bisexual and was once arrested on a morals charge in a Santa Monica, California, restroom.

.

Gregory Hemingway, the author Ernest's youngest son, died of hypertension and heart disease five days after being arrested in Florida for sitting on a roadside curb, naked, trying to put on a dress and high heels. During the 1970s he had been a practicing physician, at some point had undergone a sex-change operation and was now known as Gloria, according to Reuters. She was found dead in a private cell of the Miami-Dade Women's Detention Center.

.

When **Terrence McNally**'s *Corpus Christi* was performed shortly before X-myth at the University of Northern Iowa in the Bible Belt, a Republican state senator complained that the stage paid for with tax dollars should not be used to perform something about "Jesus the king of queers." The students, however, did perform the play, and when the head of the theater department was asked if he would allow a play that portrayed **Muhammad** in a way offensive to Muslims, or **Gautama**, or **Abraham**, **Steve Taft** responded, "I'd have to read the play. Then we'd see."

.

"If God Hates Fags (I Hate God)" is one of the titles of a queercore rap combo known as **Ninja Death Squad**. Their *CD* is called *Appreciate Our Art* (Heartcore).

.

Admiral Chester W Nimitz Jr, son of the admiral who headed the World War Two Pacific Ocean operations, and his wife Joan were non-believers who in their late eighties were in deteriorating health. Together, they chose to take their own lives after a marriage of 62 years. One of the admiral's sisters, a nun, was very unhappy about this, but *Newsweek*'s **Anna Quindlen** wrote a refreshingly positive editorial about euthanasia (February 4, 2002). The press, as usual, did not report that the Nimitzes were freethinkers.

.

Generally overlooked is that **Leos Janácek** (1854 - 1928), the composer born in Hukvaldy, Czech Republic, was a non-theist. He is known for having developed a Czech folksong tradition, writing several operas, a mass, instrumental chamber pieces, and song cycles. But, according to the *Grove Dictionary of Music*

(2001), "Conventional religion meant little to him. As his wife recorded, he never went to church, never prayed, and paid no attention to his children's religious upbringing. The liturgical pieces of his student days are some of his dullest and least individual."

.

Asked to define a humanist, the author of *Oh! Calcutta*, **Kenneth Tynan** (1927 - 1980), according to a recent biography, said, "A humanist is someone who remembers the faces of the people he spanks."

.

A prostitute in **V S Naipaul**'s *Half a Life*, angry that her client was taking so long, pleaded, "Fuck like an Englishman."

.

The eminent paleontologist and non-theist **Stephen Jay Gould** makes it all so clear: "We are here because one odd group of fishes had a peculiar fin anatomy that could transform into legs for terrestrial creatures; because the earth never froze entirely during an ice age; because a small and tenuous species, arising in Africa a quarter of a million years ago, has managed, so far, to survive by hook and by crook. We may yearn for a 'higher' answer - but none exists."

Summer 2002

George Gershwin was gay. That's what **Irving Caesar** told **Lyle Stuart** long ago. You read it here first. According to Stuart, it's one of Hollywood's and New York's best-kept secrets.

While Gershwin was alive, no-one publicly discussed the subject. Outing is a recent development. For example, even when **Charles Laughton** married **Elsa Lanchester** in 1929, no-one talked about its being a contractual marriage. When Gershwin (1898-1937) died of a tumor, the subject of his love life did not come up in print, although, in private, individuals such as Caesar (who died at the age of 101 in 1996) talked about it with Stuart. The two had Manhattan offices in Tin Pan Alley's Brill Building at 1619 Broadway.

Stuart worked for *Variety* (1945-6), edited *Music Business* (1946-8), founded *Exposé* (1951), and since 1990 has been president of Barricade Books. Caesar is the lyricist who put words to "Tea for Two," "Swanee," and "Is It True What They Say About Dixie?"

Stuart, who has just published my *Celebrities in Hell* (Barricade Books, 288 pages, paperback, $14.95), asked after the book came out why I hadn't included Gershwin. I told him that I could document brother Ira's atheism, for **Ira Gershwin** had told **Michael Feinstein** after George's death at such a young age that he would gladly have died in George's place if he could have. And, added Feinstein, "for the rest of his life [Ira] never believed in God." Meanwhile, one can only speculate about George's views concerning monotheism.

"You knew George was gay?" Stuart casually asked. I was nonplussed. One of my all-time favorite composers was gay, the person who wrote "The Man I Love" and "Rhapsody in Blue"?

What Caesar had told Stuart is that showbiz cognoscenti knew about Gershwin's homosexuality, but the subject was not written about, in order to protect important people's reputations. George was only one of many whose sexual orientation was not mentioned and, in fact, still remains secret.

However, according to Caesar, George's "beard" was **Esther Sillabee**, at one time a publicist for the bandleader **Vincent Lopez** and also for the **Plaza Hotel**. It is difficult to find anything in print about her, but she has been credited with having discovered **Gregory Peck**.

Esther dated George, Caesar told Stuart, in order that he could be seen with a female companion. But once, when he was half an hour late to an appointment at the Brill Building, in anger she blurted out something like "you dirty Jew-bastard," whereupon George ended it. Cut his beard, a wag could say.

Skeptics about all this, of course, will retort by singing George's own "It Ain't Necessarily So." A pity that Oscar Levant died in 1972 without revealing what he knew, which could have confirmed all this - and could even have been self-incriminating.

.

Ian McKellen

"And what do you do?" **Sir Ian McKellen** asked. "I'm an author," I replied.

We were at the annual ceremonial of the **American Academy of Arts and Letters**, the 250-member honorary group of notable American artists, writers and composers, which also includes 74 foreign members (e.g., **Margaret Drabble, Thom Gunn, David Hockney**). Presumably, Sir Ian thought I might be a member or a recipient of one of the Academy's awards. The ceremonial, which I attend as a journalist, is not open to the general public. When I explained that I have written two books about people who have not been attracted to organized religion, he said with a smile, "Is *anyone* any more?"

When I mentioned writing for the present journal, Sir Ian expressed deep interest, asked how to subscribe, and exchanged e-mail addresses. Not wanting to monopolize him, I started to leave but he eyed my 36-year-old black friend, **Peter Ross**, and brought him into the conversation, too. How much longer can the Catholic Church continue? Sir Ian wondered aloud, commenting upon all the reports about priests sexually abusing children. He then turned to the subject of computers, and my cybergeek friend and I talked about OS X, gigabytes, and digital imaging.

It was only when I returned home that I realized I'd listed this incredibly handsome man in my *Who's Who in Hell* (Barricade Books) as well as in my just-published *Celebrities in Hell* (Barricade Books), documenting that he is an atheist who considers Hell simply a theological invention.

Tortola is anything but a Caribbean paradise, according to **Purnell Christian**, a young man living with HIV/AIDS. To **Dr Richard Stern**, director of the Central American Agua Buena Human Rights Association (rastern@racsa.co.cr), Mr. Christian said that when he was found to have AIDS he was fired from a civil service job he had held for eight years.

Then he was asked to return accrued pension funds. According to UN AIDS statistics, more than 400,000 people are HIV+ in the Caribbean region. Purnell, who is a graduate of Cornell University, cannot find a job and cannot afford the anti-retroviral medications. "You lose all your dignity when you are not allowed to work," Purnell told Dr Stern. Attempts to reach a spokesperson for the territory, of which **Queen Elizabeth II** has been the official head of state since 1952, have been unsuccessful.

.

"Locals tell you that birds fly over the city using only one wing, the other covering their posterior," **Tim Reid** of the London *Times* has written, according to the *New York Post*. In Afghanistan, Kandahar's Pashtuns for centuries are said to have practiced homosexuality, and now that America's don't-ask-don't-tell Army has taken over they see heavily bearded men walking the streets with clean-shaven fresh-faced (and usually poverty-stricken) boys.

Craig S Smith in *The New York Times* confirmed that the puritanical Taliban tried hard but were unsuccessful in fighting paedophilia. The present government has issued a directive barring "beardless boys" - a euphemism for underage sex partners - from police stations, military bases and commanders' compounds. Chocolate is a major lure, the reporter found. A Manhattan wag wonders where the reporter got the chocolate.

.

Ex-President **Richard Nixon**'s private views about Jews were shockingly anti-Semitic, but his views on gays are also raising eyebrows. Recently released tapes reveal his having said, "You know what happened to the Greeks. Homosexuality destroyed them. Sure, **Aristotle** was a homo. We all know that. So was Socrates. The last six Roman emperors were fags. Now that's what happened to Britain." As for Californians, he reportedly told aides, "I won't shake hands with anybody from San Francisco."

.

American politicians are not known for their profundity. **Anne Robinson**, the acerbic British quiz-show gal, has been quoted as observing that at a benefit concert she saw **President George W Bush** wave to **Stevie Wonder**, so we can only guess what views about gays are held by the person who majored in history at Yale and earned C's. In 1982 the AIDS activist and non-theist Larry Kramer called New York's ex-**Mayor Ed Koch** "a closeted gay man," according to **Boze Hadleigh**'s titillating and must-read *In Or Out, Stars on Sexuality* (London: Fusion Press, 2001).

So are *we* to blame for what goes on in our governing circles? Yes, as illustrated in 1899 by **Charles C Moore**'s being the last known American to have been imprisoned for blasphemy - imprisoned for having sent atheistic materials through the mails, he received a hero's welcome when he returned home. It became a time when the American public no longer would put up with the irrational idea of "treason against God." As the American journalist **James Reston** astutely has observed, "All politics are based on the indifference of the majority."

Autumn 2002

Two works featuring gay freethinkers are currently wowing Broadway: *The Goat, or Who is Sylvia?*, the Tony-winning drama by **Edward Albee**; and *Hairspray*, in which **Harvey Fierstein** plays Mrs Edna Turnblad in **John Waters**'s camp classic about teen angst.

A nominal Quaker and pacifist but not a Trinitarian, **Edward Albee** writes about an architect with a secret. The secret is not that the architect has a (handsome) homosexual son. It's that he has fallen for Sylvia because of "those eyes of hers." His wife reacts by throwing furniture all over the place, and the son as referee in one scene attempts to get close to his father, then draws back as if it would be inappropriate to kiss a father who knows his son is gay. So is it *The Two Gentlemen of Verona*'s Sylvia "that all our swains commend her?/Holy, fair, and wise is she;/The heaven such grace did lend her"? No, the architect has fallen in love with a goat. Whatsay? Posing such a question is analogous to asking if **Hamlet**'s is a real or a figurative ghost.

The audience never really gets to see a physical goat, so whatever is contained in the cloth bag dragged in during a final scene could be explicated in different ways. For one, the architect appears to be highly moral but is experiencing something in life that he feels should not be, and Albee is clever enough not to provide a clear meaning of what that something is.

At the play's conclusion, the *real* play continues as theatergoers speculate concerning Albee's purpose or message. If we can't absolutely figure it out, so much the better - that's Albee. If we think the "sin" is that the architect has fallen for a prostitute, a transsexual, an effeminate gay, or the neighbor's wife or daughter, are we simply revealing our own Sylvia? Whatever or whoever Sylvia is, the solid marriage described at the beginning is in trouble.

Meanwhile, the play has many funny moments (starting with the outrageous title and the play's premise). Ideal family life is satirized, and disillusionment with people in power is developed. Upon leaving the theater, playgoers feel they have seen a cutting-edge Greek tragedy. The problem is to try to put into words what has excited the feelings of pity and terror. A lady I conversed with afterwards detested the very idea of a man's having sex with a goat, so Sylvia will be interpreted literally by some, depending upon whatever evolutionary level they've reached.

.

In my *Celebrities in Hell* (Barricade Books, 2002), I quote **Harvey Fierstein** as saying on the Public Broadcasting System that he is both a cultural Jew and an atheist. In one of the gayest of all plays, *Hairspray*, he also is one of the funniest women *ever* to appear on a Broadway stage! He doesn't play the role as if he were a man pretending to be a woman. In his own hoarse voice (related to a childhood accident), he openly plays a woman, the one Divine played in the 1988 movie on which the musical is based.

Fierstein adroitly dances in and wears a wig that weighs almost 3 kilograms, a dress that weighs 4 kilograms, padding that weighs over 16 kilograms, and says, "the lashes alone can kill you!" The setting is Baltimore of the 1960s, home of the movie's author, **John Waters** ("the king of bad taste," who still delights in bragging that he was arrested in 1965 for smoking pot in his New York University dorm room). It comes lovingly alive in this bawdy old-fashioned musical that praises fat girls (much as **George Bernard Shaw** praised **Gladys Homfrey** in 1894) and has led to department stores featuring *Hairspray*-like bouffant wigs and iridescent paisley clothing with feathers for chubby gals. The dancing, by a troupe of blacks and whites that includes a boy with a duck's-ass hairdo, is outstanding.

The story involves a fat girl's success in show business, racial integration being promoted, and the humanistic message that we all need to have pride in who we are. On their cutesy homepage, you can see and hear the stunning cast.

.

Martin Duberman is the non-believer and humanist who wrote "Gayness Becomes You" in *The Nation* (20 May 2002). Author in

1996 of *Stonewall*, one of the better works describing the 1969 riots on behalf of human rights by homosexuals, he is a distinguished professor of history at the City University of New York and founder of the Center for Lesbian and Gay Studies (CLAGS).

Dr Duberman explains that, despite enormous variations in their lifestyles, gays view gender, sexuality, primary relationships, friendship and family quite differently now from what they did fifty years ago, when **Herbert Marcuse** suggested they (the term then was homosexuals) might provide a cutting-edge social critique of vast importance one day. Today, one hears that gay differentness is not just a defensible variation "but a decided advance over mainstream norms, that gay subcultural perspectives could richly inform conventional life, could open up an unexplored range of human possibilities for *everyone*."

That is, *if* the mainstream were listening, but it isn't. It isn't because the mainstream's antenna "remains tuned to a limited number of false frequencies: that heterosexuality is the Natural Way; that (as we move right of center) lifetime monogamous pair-bonding is the likeliest guarantee of human happiness; that the gender binary (everyone is either male *or* female and each gender has distinctive characteristics) is rooted in biology." The mainstream persists in thinking that gays need to be barred because they consist of overweight butch dykes, foul-mouthed black queers, dickless "men" and surgically created "women" delusionally convinced that they're part of some non-existent group called the "transgendered." In other words, the more different the outsider, "the greater the threat posed to its own lofty sense of blue-ribbon superiority. Fraternizing with true exotics can prove dangerously seductive, opening up Normal People to possibilities within themselves that they prefer to keep under lock and key."

Dr Duberman differs entirely, of course, but makes it clear what gays are up against these days. Despite the mainstream's view, he advises that gays continue being themselves because "gayness becomes you." One of his personal heroes is **Emma Goldman**, the anarchist, advocate of birth control, and fellow non-believer. She also believed that each generation needs to discard "the burdens of the past, which hold us all in a net." Or,

72

as the humanist **Somerset Maugham** advised in *Of Human Bondage*, determine what your bondages are and discard them unless they are physical.

.

Alan Riding, writing in *The New York Times* about a **Michelangelo** exhibition at the Casa Buonarroti in Florence, tells about *The Rape of Ganymede*, which Michelangelo gave to twelve-year-old **Tommaso de Cavalieri** in 1532 when the artist was 57: "Letters between Michelangelo and Tommaso hint at no particular anguish. In early-16th-century Florence, it seems, intimate relationships between men and boys were not uncommon." Riding makes no mention that Michelangelo was rumored to have had sex with **Pope Julius III**.

.

A little-known Manhattan, uh, theophagist, **Allen Windsor**, has been advising theists how they should sip wine at their monotheistic Eucharists.

"Swallow very, very quickly," he says, "before the miracle of transubstantiation takes place. Otherwise, I hope y'know what you'll end up swallowing"!

Winter 2002

Harry Hay's death at the age of 90 in Los Angeles reminds one that, long before the 1969 Stonewall riots, Hay in 1950-51, with **Rudi Gernreich**, **Robert Hull**, **Chuck Rowland** and **Dale Jennings,** founded the **Mattachine Society** (for masked people, unknown and anonymous). This led to the formation of several chapters for homosexuals and, in 1953, to the founding of *One*, a magazine that gained a circulation of 5,000.

Will Geer, the actor who was one of Harry's lovers and who played Grandpa Walton on *TV*, had been the one who introduced Hay to communist organizing. Together they worked on a general strike that closed the Port of San Francisco in 1934. A disaffected Roman Catholic, Hay co-founded the **Radical Faeries**, but was ousted when during a parade he carried a NAMBLA sign. His partner of 40 years, **John Burnside**, survives.

•

Readers have been helpful in suggesting the names of non-believers who are not included in my two books, *Who's Who in Hell* and Celebrities in Hell (Barricade Books). In any second editions, for example, the following is a partial listing (good as well as bad guys) of who might be included along with over 10,000 previously named. Known gays are designated with a symbolic ass-to-risk. If you know otherwise, please e-mail me.

- Activist: *****Harry Hay**, early American proponent of gay rights, humanist.
- Artists: *****Anthony Blunt**, British art   historian turned Soviet spy, non-theist; **Thomas Eakins**, realist painter, non-theist.
- Authors: **Roddy Doyle**, Irish novelist, non-   theist; **Deborah Garrison**, poet, humanist; **Theodore Geisel** (*Dr Seuss*), humanist; **Nadine Gordimer**, South   African novelist, humanist; **Gene Roddenberry**, science-fiction writer, humanist;

Salman Rushdie, non-theist; **Studs Terkel**, non-theist; **Peter Theroux**, non-theist; **Alice Walker**, humanist.
- Business: **Ted Turner**, founder of *CNN*, non-theist.
- Cartoons: **Charles Schultz**, humanist; **Tom Toles**, humanist.
- City planning: **Sir Peter Hall**, non-theist.
- Feminism: **Oriana Fallaci**, Italian journalist, non-theist; **Gloria Steinem**, author, non-theist.
- Government: **Idi Amin**, Ugandan dictator, "Conqueror of the British Empire," atheist;
    Roberto D'Aubuisson, hated El Salvadoran rightist, non-theist; **Fernando Henrique Cardoso**, ex-President of Brazil, a non-believer; **Nicolae Ceausescu**, communist dictator of Romania, 1965-89, atheist; **Carlo Azeglio Ciampi**, President of the Italian Republic, non-theist; **Ricardo Lagos Escobar**,
    Chile's President, a socialist agnostic; **Slobodan Milosevic**, ex-Yugoslavian President, atheist; **Pol Pot**, leader in Cambodia of Khmer Rouge guerrillas, atheist; **Jonas Savimbi**, Angolan guerrilla leader, non-theist.
- History: **Robin Lane Fox**, Biblical critic, non-theist.
- Journalism: **Hendrik Hertzberg**, *New Yorker* writer, non-theist.
- Movies: **Orla Brady**, atheist; ***Arthur Dong**, *Family Fundamentals*, non-theist; ***Rainer Werner Fassbinder**, non-theist; **Gael Garcia Bernal**, priest in *Padre Amaro*, atheist; **Stanley Kramer**, humanist; **Marcel Marceau**, humanist; **Tim Robbins**, humanist; **Susan Sarandon**, humanist; **Oliver Stone**, humanist; **Julia Sweeney**, non-theist.
- Music: ***Leonard Bernstein**, humanist; ***George Gershwin**, "The Man I Love," non-believer; **Marilyn Manson**, humanist; **Yoko Ono**, humanist; **Brad Roberts** of Crash Test Dummies, non-theist.
- Scientist: **Rita Levi Montalcini**, Nobel laureate.
- Sport: **Ted Williams**, baseball star, atheist.

- Television: **Phil Donahue**, humanist; **Will Geer** (Zeb "Grandpa" Walton), non-theist; **Al Lewis** ("Grandpa Munster"), humanist; **Louis Theroux**, English TV presenter, non-theist.

Humanist journals generally have been critical of my not having written specifically for their vested interests, resulting in criticisms that focused on their own narrow editorial slant. To date, neither book has yet been disinterestedly evaluated by a critic who discerned the international scope of the two books and their attempt to picture the state of non-theism at the end of the twentieth century. What a pity that **Nicolas Walter** died just before the books were published, although he did read an early draft of the first, suggesting some profound inclusions.

Will second editions of the books ever come out? In light of my having received so little help from the major rationalist and humanist organizations, few readers have been aware that the project needs input. In short, Harvard's Houghton Library is receiving my (and also **Gore Vidal**'s) correspondence, but the task of future listings appears now to be best handled by **Celebrity Atheists**.

.

Paul Rudnick, the gay non-theistic author of *Jeffrey*, upon hearing the Hollywood deal-maker **Michael Ovitz**'s complaint that a "gay mafia" was largely responsible for engineering his downfall, wrote in the *New Yorker* that "Lieutenants in the Gay Mafia are usually heavily armed, especially during tank-top season" and "the Gay Mafia's links to the Catholic Church are extensive and most often begin with the phrase, 'Jimmy, did you know that the Apostles liked to wrestle?' "

.

Sir Ian McKellen was the only non-theist of two dozen celebrities selected by readers of *Metrosource NY* in a "Special People We Love in 2002" balloting.

.

Manhattan's Chelsea men are shocked that **Bono** is reported in major newspapers as saying of **Sting**'s anatomy that he has, uh, no visible means for procreation.

Spring 2003

A major gay non-believer and composer has died. **Lou Harrison** (14 May 1917 - 2 February 2003), a member of the American Academy of Arts and Letters, had survived diabetes, a triple bypass surgical operation and the death of his long-time partner, **William Colvig**. However, he never recovered consciousness after stumbling out of an automobile on his way to a dinner in Indiana.

Like his mentor **Virgil Thomson**, another gay non-believer, Harrison in the mid-1940s was a critic at the *New York Herald Tribune* but never much liked the city. He was happiest in California, where in 1992 he wrote me that he was certain "like my father before me, that 'when you're dead you're dead,' and simply turned off - all systems down." He added that he had talked about **Epicurus** to his local humanist group, liked the writings of **Lucretius**, was enormously opposed to organized religion, "and feel that the Christians and Muslims are responsible for uncountable human and other beings' miseries."

His openly gay book, *Joys and Perplexities: Selected Poems*, was published in 1997, but he will be remembered for his musical works that combined Asian, particularly Javanese, and American styles.

·

A major work can now be added to the gay canon: **Vern L. Bullough**'s *Before Stonewall, Activists for Gay and Lesbian Rights in Historical Context* (NY, London, Oxford: Harrington Park Press, 2002).

Before Stonewall is an essential source for understanding one of the most inspiring human rights campaigns of our time. What surprises the reader is that intimate details from five decades in the past have for the first time been collected from seventeen women, seventeen men and Christine Jorgensen about key individuals who fought for gay and lesbian rights. Credit goes to **Dr Vern L. Bullough**, currently an adjunct professor of nursing at the University of Southern California, who took over the project conceived by **Wayne Dynes** nearly a decade ago but who withdrew because of other commitments and difficulties with potential contributors.

In an introduction, Bullough surveys the historical context. He underlines the importance of **Karl Heinrich Ulrichs** (1825-95), who argued in Germany that same-sex relationships are no more dangerous to society than procreative sex between married persons. **Karoly Maria Benkert** (or Kertbeny) (1824-82) is credited for having coined the term "homosexuality." **Richard von Krafft-Ebing** (1840-1902) helped bring homosexuality out of the closet. **Magnus Hirschfeld** (1868-1935) worked to remove German laws against homosexuality.

Although **Emma Goldman** (1869-1940) urged Marxists to change laws concerning gays, the Russian Communist Party under Stalin considered homosexuality a product of capitalist degeneration. The Nazis sent thousands to their deaths in concentration camps and destroyed Hirschfeld's research materials. Bullough concisely details what homosexuals painfully endured in other parts of the world, tells of the "pansy craze" in the 1920s, and mentions the importance of works by **Radclyffe Hall**, **Blair Niles**, **Robert Scully**, even **James T. Farrell**. He points out the liberating elements of Britain's Wolfenden Report and the inspiring help supplied to individuals by the American Civil Liberties Union.

The book is divided into four parts: pre-1950; organizational activists; movers and shakers on the national scene; and other voices and their influence.

Henry Gerber is dubbed the grandfather of the American gay movement, his problems with the Establishment vividly described by **Jim Kepner** and **Stephen O. Murray**. Other pre-1950 activists include **Xavier Mayne**, **Prescott Townsend**, **Jeannette Foster**, **Pearl Hart**, **Lisa Ben** and **Berry Berryman**. **C. A. Tripp** writes a lucid description of the positive role played by sexologist **Alfred *C.* Kinsey**.

Harry Hay, **Del Martin**, **Phyllis Lyon** are three of the organizational activists described in detail, along with others of those who formed the Mattachine Society and ONE, Inc. **Dale Jennings** was one of the first who admitted their homosexuality; he then successfully fought a public charge of lewd behavior. **Jim Kepner** decried ego-driven antagonisms among organizers, but with **Dorr Legg** and others created the first gay-studies program - the first after Hirschfeld's institute was torched by the Nazis 23 years earlier.

Franklin Kameny, head of the Mattachine Society in the capital, was among the first to proclaim that homosexuality is neither sick nor immoral, and he came up with the slogan *Gay is Good*.

In 1955, individuals involved in the Daughters of Bilitis and the publication *Ladder* are credited. **Barbara Gittings**, **Sten Russell**, **Helen Sanders**, **Billye Talmadge** and **Barbara Grier** are some of the many whose efforts are described.

The times, they were a-changing. Magazines, little by little, showed pictures of naked men, the movies became less prudish. *The Advocate* in 1968 had a section selling sex, classified as well as unclassified. **Hugh Heffner**'s *Playboy* similarly began treating sex behavior openly.

The "other voices" in the final part of the book include descriptions of the parts played by **Allen Ginsberg**, **Donald Webster Cory**, **Christine Jorgensen**, **Troy Perry** and others.

A scorecard is almost needed to keep track of which women slept with other activist women, which men with other activist men, and who else did what to whom. The various brief biographies refreshingly dish the dirt. The book's negatives are next to nil. The index is commendably thorough.

Today, "Stonewall" to most is a reference to the June 1969 Greenwich Village uprising, in which I was a participant. However, from a historical context, June 1969 was but a minor part of the picture. Today's various veterans' groups are, sadly, a fissiparous lot whose members may or may not have played any role in the ugly disturbances that week in June. They uninspiringly fight over which group gets to lead the annual Heritage of Pride Parade, and they disagree about how to raise money and where to spend it. What *Before Stonewall* points out is that the gay and lesbian rights movement has been a long time coming, from Europe no less, but its pre-1950 activists here and elsewhere are deserving of an updated appreciation for their activism, efforts that have resulted in the gay life that so many of us now enjoy and that countless others are still unable to experience.

.

Michael Jackson, raised a Jehovah's Witness, is not happy that another witness - thirteen-year-old J. Chandler - has charged him in a four-page declaration that neither person wishes had been leaked

www.thesmokinggun.com/archive/mjcivil1.html

That website also contains shocking mugshots of *VIPs* who wish they had not been included. These are cybernetic times in which, if you let it all hang out, you can end up a hangdog.

Summer 2003

Alan Cumming, Scotland's gift to Yankee showbiz, is available, guys! According to Rush & Molloy in the *Daily News*, he has split with theater director **Nick Philippo**, and the two live apart, although remaining as partners in The Art Party, their theater company.

When Cumming started at the Royal Scottish Academy of Music and Drama in Glasgow, he met his future professional partner (**Forbes Masson**) and his wife (**Hilary Lyons**, whom he divorced after eight years of marriage). His career has grown to the point that he is a superstar, both in Hollywood and on Broadway.

In a recent *Village Voice* column by fellow freethinker **Michael Musto**, Cumming laughs about how he wore no underwear during a stunt rehearsal for the movie, *X-2: X-Men United*, in which he plays Nightcrawler and which scored the fourth-biggest opening ever with an estimated $85.9 million. He then found four grown men, on their knees, getting cameras ready for a back shot, "staring and poking at my behind. I think to myself that I have never had so many gentlemen this concerned with that area of my body." In 1998-9, when he starred on Broadway in *Cabaret*, many more than four in my front row alone were staring at that area.

Cumming currently is working on a TV show, *Mr and Mr Nash*, which he has described as "a sort of gay *Hart to Hart*. I'm the mischievous one who gets into all the scrapes."

In my *Celebrities in Hell* (Barricade Books), I quote his telling an *Interview* reporter that as a youth he was forced to attend church, but now "I'm completely atheist. I don't hold any beliefs about God and stuff. And I can't do the church thing."

.

The Crimson Letter: Harvard, Homosexuality and the Shaping of American Culture (St Martin's Press, 2003) tells how the university shaped the future of a number of eminent American gay and/or bisexual freethinkers, including conductor, pianist and composer **Leonard Bernstein**; novelist **Frank O'Hara**; architect **Philip Johnson**; the bisexual sexologist **Alfred Kinsey**; philosopher, poet, and novelist **George Santayana**, and others.

The author, **Douglass Shand-Tucci**, points out that, until the twentieth century, Boston was *the* intellectual capital, *the* place for intellectual excitement, a city where the Bohemian lifestyle flourished. Harvard's use of Socratic tutorials such as those at Oxford and Cambridge encouraged close teacher-student relations, and Shand-Tucci cites examples of how gays collaborated and formed friendships at a time in which homosexuality was considered a crime.

Bernstein had an affair with **Dimitri Mitropoulos** in Boston and, later in New York, with **Aaron Copland**, eventually marrying and having children. The book contains other interesting titbits.

.

Hairspray, still the hottest ticket on Broadway, was the big winner when the Drama Desk gave out its annual awards. **Harvey Fierstein**, its star in drag, was the big winner. In *Celebrities in Hell*, Fierstein is quoted as having said on Uncensored, a public broadcasting system, that he was both a cultural Jew and an atheist.

.

The British author *D. H.* Lawrence is buried in Westminster Abbey, right? No, years after the novelist's death, his wife, **Frieda**, had his remains disinterred from a grave in Vence, France, cremated, and returned to San Cristobal, New Mexico. In the 1920s, the couple had spent fifteen months on 160 wooded acres there that had been given by his patron, **Mabel Dodge Luhan**, in exchange for the original manuscript of *Sons and Lovers*. Lawrence once had described the New Mexico site thus: "Ah! It was beauty, beauty absolute, at any hour of the day."

 Visitors to the area would agree, for the area thirteen miles north of Taos is a perfect hiding place for a person known as believing that industrial culture dehumanizes. The village of San Cristobal is off the main road and now, as then, has few facilities. He would have traveled nearby to Taos, seeing the Pueblo people who were skilled in making drums, moccasins and leatherwork items. He would have found their spicy food a joy, would have watched dancers at powwows, and would have walked to and around the foothills of his ranch.

Frieda is said to have feared that some of his admirers might find his "cremains" and scatter them across the ranch, so a shrine was built in which his ashes were mixed in with concrete used to build the memorial.

My own *Who's Who in Hell* (Barricade, 2000) quotes Lawrence's telling his biographer, **Richard Aldington**, "I believe the nearest I have come to perfect love was with a young coal miner when I was about sixteen."

Aldington added: "I should say Lawrence was about 85% hetero and 15% homo." Frieda was aware, refusing to allow a farmer's boy, William Henry, into their house. Biographer **Brenda**

Maddox, however, thought that Lawrence was deeply attracted to men but was repelled by homosexuals.

Lawrence's love life is now becoming further uncemented. Playwright **Larry Kramer**, a freethinking humanist like Lawrence, has been talking and writing about how *Women in Love* had a chapter in which Rupert and Gerald are lovers, one that was not published. In a recent *DVD* release of *Women in Love* (*MGM* Home Video) and *Women in Love, and Other Dramatic Writings* (Grove Press), Kramer researches Lawrence in detail, finding he had many attachments to men.

.

The Times now includes photos and stories of people getting married. The May 4 issue included a photo of non-believer **Tony Kushner**, 46, marrying **Mark Harris**, 39. The author of *Angels in America* and the editor-at-large for *Entertainment Weekly* affirmed their partnership at a restaurant, Gabriel's, before 150 guests who included film director **Mike Nichols**; television host **Diane Sawyer**; actresses **Linda Emond** and **Kathleen Chalfant**; director **George C. Wolfe**; and playwright and non-believer **Larry Kramer**.

.

Dan Savage, the non-believer and sex-advice columnist, is so infuriated by Republican Senator **Rick Santorum**'s equating homosexuality with polygamy and incest that he is searching for a new connotation for "santorum."

The sticky fecal stuff after anal intercourse, for example, could be described: "To my embarrassment, there on the sheet was some ugly santorum." Savage thinks the name of the senator from Pennsylvania needs to become part of the English language, and he is asking for other suggestions to make sure Santorum is not soon forgotten.

Autumn 2003

The 34th annual gay parade in June lasted more than five hours and went from Manhattan's Fifth Avenue at 52nd Street past St Patrick's Cathedral ("Shame, shame!" many marchers shouted, pointing at the structure) to the Hudson River in Greenwich Village.

Marchers were jubilant about Canada's just-announced decision to allow same-sex marriages. Their placards had much to say about the United States Supreme Court's recent ruling that struck down laws against sodomy in all 50 states.

Joked freethinker **John Waters**, the filmmaker whom **William Burroughs** once dubbed "the pope of trash," "It's amazing to me that the court even had to rule on sodomy. Middle America is now going, 'Wow, we *never* did that. Want to try *that* tonight?' "

.

My article, "Gay in the 1960s - the time was ripe for revolution," was featured in *The Villager* (18 June 2003; also, it is found at the end of the present book) and discussed the uprising at the Stonewall bar that inspired others to fight back against homophobia. To see a rare photo of the Stonewall Inn's 1969 bar price list of $1 drinks, go to

http://www.thevillager.com/villager_8/gayinthe60.html

.

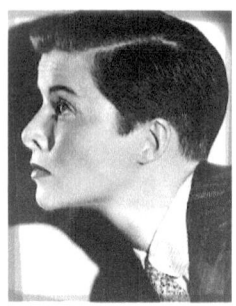

Katharine Hepburn - who once told a reporter, "I'm an atheist, and that's it" - might have been, even probably was, a double-gater. Tabloids are writing that the late lover of **Spencer Tracy** likely had a sexual connection with **Cynthia McFadden**, an *NBC* news correspondent who now is executor of Hepburn's estate.

There was a 50-year difference in their ages, however, leading *Daily News* gossip columnists **George Rush** and **Joanna Molloy** to claim that Cynthia was more like Hepburn's daughter. Just the same, throughout her life rumors abounded about the slacks "Jimmy," as she called herself when young, wore and the women companions she had.

Meanwhile, most considered that her husband (a college beau, **Ludlow Ogden Smith**) was more like a brother, one who knew about her affairs with **Howard Hughes**, **George Stevens**, **John Ford** and her agent, **Leland Hayward**.

A. Scott Berg's just-published *Kate Remembered*, dedicated to his companion, **Kevin McCormick**, is not particularly liked by **Robert Gottlieb**, a former editor of the *New Yorker*, who complains that "surely the world doesn't need to know what Hepburn felt about her friend's personal life.

And - far more serious - was it a favor to his beloved Hepburn to expose to the world Irene's [**Irene Mayer Selznick**, the wife of David O] late conclusions about 'Sister Kate's' sexual nature?" Selznick had once found Hepburn in an exchange "that suggested a level of intimacy she had never allowed herself to believe," and speculates about **Dorothy Arzner**, **Phyllis Wilbourn**, **Laura Harding**, and **Nancy Hamilton**.

Berg reports that Hepburn drank King William IV Scotch, first filling the glass beyond the brim with ice, then pouring a shot slowly over the cubes, then topping it with soda. When **Cole Porter** visited, Hepburn remembered fondly, he "used to come to this house, and he'd straighten pictures for five minutes before he'd even sit down." On the mantel of her East Side apartment she had a pair of small figurines for which she once had posed - in the nude!

She once complained about **Stephen Sondheim**, her neighbor, who had many gentlemen callers and played the piano too loudly. Her father was a urologist who treated venereal diseases, her mother an activist for legal birth control who battled for women's suffrage in Connecticut.

Accounts of Hepburn's death failed to mention her atheism or that, when she was thirteen, she discovered her teenage brother, Tom, had hanged himself. She had said, "In a state of numb shock I cut him down and laid him on the bed." The police, however, said the brother's feet had hit the ground and he had had to pull hard against the torn bed sheet to deliberately strangle himself, that Hepburn had attempted to hold the body upright, that she was supporting his body in her arms when the doctor arrived.

"I had heard that maybe a girl had rejected him - who knows, maybe a boy. Whatever it was, he simply could not cope," Kate wondered. Dr Hepburn, in an attempt to get journalists not to call it a suicide, said this son's death was the result of an extremely unfortunate boyish stunt.

Two days later, the doctor's brother was found dead in a garage where his car's engine was running. Hepburn downplayed the suicide of her mother's father, of her father's brother, of her father's own oldest brother and of her brother with, "They simply did not believe in moaning about anything."

Hepburn's "love" for the married and Catholic **Spencer Tracy** was public knowledge, even to Tracy's Episcopalian wife. When Tracy in 1963 had a pulmonary crisis, the two women took turns sitting at his bedside. Hepburn once described their "twenty-seven years together in what was to me absolute bliss." Her living to the age of 96 at least proves that any genetic disposition towards committing suicide was not in her script.

.

Marlon Brando, the 79-year-old actor and freethinker, is said to have had a one-nighter with novelist **Paula Fox** in the 1940s. Their allegedly illegitimate daughter, psychologist **Linda Carroll**, is claiming in a forthcoming book that Brando's DNA will prove the liaison. If so, Brando has a Love grandchild, for Carroll's daughter is **Courtney Love**.

In the past, Brando has admitted to siring nine children (uh, none with Wally "Mr Peepers" Cox), the youngest being around eight years old. Rush and Molloy, in a New York *Daily News* column, write, "If the claim is true, Brando would be the great-grandfather of **Frances Bean**, 11, Love's child with her late husband, Nirvana front man **Kurt Cobain**."

Meanwhile, Doubleday Books claims there is nothing in Carroll's book proposal about Brando, and that there "is no truth to the suggestion that she is related to Brando." Love, whose credit card was stolen and maxed out in August because a thief spent $15K at Chanel without her knowledge, has reportedly signed a $10 million deal with Virgin. That's Virgin Records, not the airline on which she was arrested last February for allegedly being "verbally abusive" to the crew.

.

Alan Cumming, the freethinker who had been living in a 430-square-foot second-floor studio on 14th Street, has purchased a $1.925 million 2,254-square-foot condo with an additional 974-square-foot wraparound terrace in the area north of Greenwich Village known as Chelsea. He bought it with his former longtime boyfriend, **Nick Philippou**, but the two have separated (see the Summer 2003 issue) and only Cumming is moving in.

.

Gays cannot legally get married here. Cartoonist **Ward Sutton** (Greenwich Village *Voice*, 12 August 2003) notes, however, that heterosexuals have no trouble getting hitched. These include strangers who have had sex once; drunks who marry in the Elvis

Chapel in Las Vegas and don't remember the ceremony; reality game show contestants who have just been introduced; wealthy elderly men and shapely young women; and repressed, self-hating gay men and oblivious women who are eager to have babies.

Sutton concludes that the sacred institution of marriage *clearly* is not meant for loving, committed, same-sex couples.

·

Brigitte Bardot, in her new book called *A Cry of Silence*, detests gay men who "jiggle their bottoms, put their little fingers in the air, and with their little castrato voices moan about what those ghastly heteros put them through." Comedians, including Manhattan drag queens at Bar d'O, complain that the ageing sexpot is wigging 'em out.

·

Philip Johnson, still gay, a nonbeliever, and 97, has signed up to construct an as-yet-unnamed nightclub on 10th Avenue and 26th Street. The dean of American architects is designing a club that will have a 50-foot-wide curved-glass wall to separate two rooms in the 6,500-square-foot former garage. No dark back rooms, of course, which no longer exist in Manhattan.

·

Joan Rivers, the acidic comic, is not mellowing in her old age. In June upon Bob Hope's death, she told the audience at Fez, "At least now his wife knows where he is." As for **Liza Minnelli**'s and **David Gest**'s separation, "I hope she has eggs left," meaning David, *Village Voice* columnist **Michael Musto** clucks. And as for her own daughter **Melissa**'s having turned down *Playboy*, "I told her, 'Ask for another $100,000 and show pussy!' I'm still paying off her wedding, and they've been divorced for a year and a half!"

·

Nonbelievers who dislike labels such as atheist, agnostic, freethinker, secularist, and humanist have come up with a new description: bright. If you're a bright (zoologist **Richard Dawkins** and Duke *U* philosopher **Daniel C Dennett** say they're brights), you are a naturalist rather than a supernaturalist and not a believer "in a physical god or heaven or angels or mysticism or theistic nonsense." The label is now drawing international interest on the Web:

http://www.the-brights.net/

.

"He's on the Down Low" is a slang expression that is understood mainly by a few in the subculture. It is code for "he's black and has a secret sexual life with men." Those who are *DL* identify themselves not as gay or bi but as black and inherently masculine.

Benoit Denizet-Lewis in *Double lives on the Down Low* (*New York Times*, 3 August 2003), describes men who lead double lives, making their wives and friends think they're straight but, to the men they're having sex with, "they're forging an exuberant new identity."

The closet, they feel, is a stifling place where fearful white people hide, whereas they don't consider themselves gay so there is nothing to "come out" to. The author points out, of course, that they're only kidding themselves. Health officials and gays everywhere fear they are spreading AIDS throughout the black community.

To balance the story, a reporter might well pen the lowdown on middle- and upper-class bisexual white and Asian men who are married and who tryst with their boy-toys.

Winter 2003

Australian-born **Leigh Bowery** is being played by **Boy George** in *Taboo* on Broadway. Meanwhile, the part of English-born **Boy George** is being played by Scottish-born **Euan Morton**. The American-born **Rosie O'Donnell**-produced musical describes them in the decadent, early 1980s, the time in London of New Romanticism. *Taboo* is quite different from the previous West End production, having been rewritten with bitchy putdowns galore by the drag diva **Charles Busch**, who is currently melodramatically starring in a movie, *Die, Mommie, Die!* In November, he was found not guilty of plagiarizing some parts of the movie's script.

The play follows Leigh and Boy George in wildly arranged club scenes, starting with "Give Me a Freak," that feature flashily dressed, stylish dancers and music that rocks the house, even the upper balconies. Depicting how Boy George rises to stardom and descends into drugs, Morton sounds, acts and looks eerily like the early George O'Dowd he is portraying. In one scene, Bowery (George himself) looks in upon four guys at a urinal, hands on each other's ass, and sings "I'll Have You All" in the vaudeville-like voice he now has. He also sings another of his own tunes, "Ich Bin Kunst," while displayed as a work of living art in a gallery window.

The 1993 **Wigstock** scene that I had the good luck to witness, in which Bowery gives birth to a baby, was conservatively repeated in *Taboo*, except this time Nicola (played by Sarah Berry) doesn't come out all bloody with umbilical cord attached.

The play has a strong ending but could not show that Bowery went on to become **Lucien Freud**'s huge naked model, who, when he died, was buried naked. Freud paid to have the body shipped back to Australia, where it was placed next to his mother's body. As if his life's show never ended, undertakers - when attempting to lower the casket with the naked corpse, which weighed 16 or 17 stones, into the ground - found the coffin was too big for the allotted space. On Broadway, at any rate, Bowery is very much alive!

Tony **Kushner**'s six-hour Broadway Tony-winning *Angels in America*, now an HBO movie, is causing as much controversy now as when it opened as a play. It excoriates President **Ronald Reagan** for his administration's slow response to the AIDS crisis. "I had friends who died in really terrible circumstances," freethinker Kushner told reporters, "because Ronald Reagan couldn't bring himself to say the word 'gay' in public till 1987."

Christopher Wilson, author of *Dancing with the Devil*, gave many blow-by-blow accounts of the **Duke and Duchess of Windsor**'s activities and those of their coterie. He reiterates in *Vanity Fair* (November 2003) that **Oscar Hammerstein's wife, Dorothy**, witnessed the Duchess of Windsor as she "play[ed] oboe" with **Jimmy Donohue** on the deck of the *RMS Queen Mary* in 1951, adding that Donohue - grandson of Woolworth's founder *F. W.* **Woolworth** - wore skirts almost as often as Wally Simpson, the duchess, did.

It was always an illusion when master illusionists **Siegfried and Roy** made 600-pound white tigers disappear. It was equally amazing to find that the elusive pair were for years among the world's openly closeted celebrities, even when Roy was seriously injured by one of the tigers. Journalists covered the story of their 44 years together rather thoroughly, except for mentioning whether or not the two are believers or freethinkers and failing to mention that **Roy Horn** and **Siegfried Fischbacher** are, according to Steve Friess in *The Advocate*, "former lovers."

Barry Manilow, writer of the Broadway-bound musical *Harmony*, found that the show's producers were short of millions of dollars and the show had to be canceled in mid-November. The show was to be about a German vaudevillian sextet, the Comedian Harmonists, during the fall of the Weimar Republic. Once asked if he believed in God, Manilow replied, "Yes, his name is **Clive Davis**, and he's the head of my record company." Asked then how important his Judaism is, he responded, "It isn't. My humanism is."

.

Sex ed formerly consisted of teachers at the chalkboard showing anatomical parts, then asking, "Any questions?" Students seldom asked anything, of course, wondering more about the teacher's sex mate. Today, teenagers trying to understand human relationships turn not to textbooks but to their *TV* sets. *Friends* covers topics like unplanned pregnancies, torn condoms, infidelity. *Joe Millionaire* includes Joe's postponing a date because of a herpes flare-up. *Sex and the City* has above-the-blankets episodes about contraception and STDs.

.

But it's ***Jerry Springer*** that brings the exceptional people out of nowhere and onto a stage to reveal their innermost secrets, show their hickies and butts, even fight in the nude. Manhattan roués look forward to *Jerry Springer the Opera* and predict that the West End production will be Broadway's next big ticket grosser.

.

Britney Spears, who sucked tongue with fellow believer **Madonna** during the Emmy awards, also educates the young about sex. In "Touch of My Hand," she sings about masturbation. Gays can empathize with her response to a *People* reporter's question about her favorite kind of kiss: "when a guy just comes up and grabs you and kisses you and makes you feel really vulnerable and does it very spontaneously."

.

Now that New York Mayor **Rudy Giuliani** is out of office, kissing - and more - is occurring in some East Village bars, particularly on weekends if you are available between 2 and 4 a.m. **Britney Spears** was seen at one on 18 November, resulting in cellphone calls that within minutes brought packs of drag queens to the place with its active dark corners.

.

Katharine Hepburn's will left $17.4 million to her heirs. Probate court records show that her four-story townhouse at 244 East

49th Street in Manhattan is being offered at $4.95 million. At her death she had $4.1 million in securities and cash, a $2.6 million trust fund, and $700,000 worth of art, furniture and other belongings. Her four-acre estate on Long Island Sound was donated to an environmental charity, and her house on the remaining three acres is on the market for $12 million. She left no money to organized religions. "I'm an atheist, and that's it," she once said.

Spring 2004

Sir Ian McKellen, one of the best-known gay humanists in the world, has been critically acclaimed for his portrayal of the good wizard Gandalf in *Return of the King*. Of the various celebrities, he looked positively regal on 29 February at this year's Oscar Award telecast, upon which he appeared as one of the presenters. Also, he joined in when the cast of the third of the *Rings* trilogy marched onto the stage to receive the eight-and-a-half-pound statuette called an Oscar.

.

What *is* a celebrity? According to **Dan Boorstin**, the ex-Librarian of Congress who died on 28 February, a celebrity is one who is well known for being well known. Boorstin also once observed, "No agnostic ever burned anyone at the stake or tortured a pagan, a heretic, or an unbeliever."

Lexicographers are known to ball around, not just sit in some library's bowels. An outspoken freethinker, lexicographer and etymologist, **Allen Walker Read**, once pointed out that in 1850 "to flash the drag" meant to wear women's clothes for immoral purposes, that in 1870 "to be in drag" meant men wearing women's costumes. He is the one who traced the origin of "O.K." (or, more likely these days, "OK") to 1839 as being a kind of joke ("all correct" purposely misspelled "oll korrect"). During World War Two, Read jotted down graffiti found in men's rooms wherever he traveled, later writing *Classic American Graffiti* (Paris, 1935). His favorite, he told fellow freethinkers in Manhattan before his death in 2002, was found on a toilet wall in Banff, Alberta, in 1928:

> Oh! I wish I had the balls of a stallion
> And a prick of a fellow I know.
> I would flee to the highest church steeple
> And I would piss on the people below.

.

Some wag spread the rumor in February during the football Super Bowl's half-time show that **Janet Jackson** had accidentally pulled **Justin Timberlake**'s pants down, exposing something small and white. But, no, a flip of one's mouse revealed the reverse, that the ugly wardrobe malfunction had exposed Janet's spangled nipple.

Meanwhile, **Blake Edwards** pointed out on 29 February that back in 1981 his fair lady, dear sweet **Julie Andrews**, had bared her breasts on screen in *S.O.B.* As to the furore Janet seemed to have caused in Puritanical America, "It was such hypocrisy," honorary Oscar recipient Edwards laughed.

·

Horizontal sex in New York City's backrooms is a thing of the past. Zippers now are supposed to stay zipped, and anyone caught on his knees is required to leave. The raunchiest bar on Manhattan's East Side, **The Cock**, is now cock- and butt-free, for smoking is not allowed either - a recent visit, for research purposes only, natch, revealed the rules were being broken after 2 a.m. Dancers in briefs continue to hoof atop the bar, the Health Department not yet having ruled that it is unsanitary to stuff money into their crotches. Those hailing the crackdown by a program called **Hotshots**, which has been formed to educate gay men about the dangers of engaging in sex with more than one person and without condoms, are now alarmed that the crackdown is leading to sex parties in private clubs that are arranged on the Internet with no supervision whatsoever.

·

Gay penguins? Holy Zeus, yes, right here in Manhattan! In the **Central Park Zoo**, Squawk and Milou, two young male chinstrap penguins, were photographed noodling on the arts and ideas page in *The Times*. And two females, Georgey and Mickey, were described as having tried to incubate eggs together. Meanwhile, Wendell and Cass, an African pair, cuddle at Coney Island's **New York Aquarium**.

Our moms and dads, the newspaper story relates, may not have told us, but over 450 animal species exhibit homosexual behavior.

·

A new **Katharine Hepburn** biography by **Darwin Porter** claims she had a lifelong romantic relationship with **Laura Harding**, the American Express heiress. And that she was with **Irene Selznick**, daughter of **Louis B. Mayer** and wife of producer **David O. Selznick**. And First Lady **Eleanor Roosevelt** sent her a series of "Oh, my darling Katharine" love letters. And allegedly the outspoken atheist's male conquests included **John Barrymore, Douglas Fairbanks Jr, Robert Mitchum, Burt Lancaster, John Ford,** and **Ernest Hemingway**.

So where was **Spencer Tracy** all this time? According to the book, with **Ingrid Bergman, Paulette Goddard, Joan Crawford, Grace Kelly** and **Nancy Davis** (who then married **Ronald Reagan**). Movie palaces appear always to have been as enticing for hetero- and bisexual thespians as churches have been for laddies and priests.

.

During Black History Month, no-one pointed out that freethinker poet **Langston Hughes** once confided to a secretary about his first homosexual experience, one initiated by a crew member on a ship that both were working on that was headed for Lagos. Biographer **Arnold Rampersad** tells how Hughes later wrote the following in *Tenerlife*:

> "Won't it hurt you?" I said.
> "Not unless it's square," he said. "Are you square?"
> "Could be," I said.
> "Let's see," he said.

.

Mikhail Baryshnikov, pictured in briefs in the *Daily News*, had wags betting the briefs had not been stuffed, that he really does have a WMD (a weapon of mass distraction).

Summer 2004

When **Jesus's father** phoned me from Canada, asking if I wanted to see his son that night in a telecast, I religiously complied. **Alan Scarfe**'s son, **Jonathan**, was excellent. As Jesus in *Judas*, he played the role handsomely, dramatically dying in the plot that S&M-ers so enjoy.

Scarfe, a Canadian who wrote an autobiography (sic) of Jack the Ripper and also is an actor, thinks, as does his son, that ethical humanism is universally imperative, that organized religion is bunk. Both should have been included in my *Who's Who in Hell* (Barricade Books, 2000) listing of more than 10,000 non-believers, for which I have profusely apologized. Now, I await a similar call from the Holy Ghost's father or, maybe, its mother.

.

Pat Tillman, who walked away from a $3.67 million football contract to enlist with his brother Kevin, then was accidentally killed by someone in his own unit during an ambush in Afghanistan, had a California memorial during which mention was made of his being with God.

"Pat isn't with God," his youngest brother Rich swore into the microphone with the *TV* cameras rolling. "He's fucking dead. He wasn't religious. So thank you for your thoughts, but he's fucking dead." Few newspapers included the outburst, but televiewers could not have missed it.

At the ceremony, Tillman's coach spoke, saying Pat once had asked him, "Could you coach gays?" The coach said yes, he could, and he had. Another speaker said the football player had read the Bible, the Qur'an, the Book of Mormon, Ralph Waldo Emerson and Henry David Thoreau. Yet another said that, at a wedding party when the bride was without a maid, Pat donned a dress and thoughtfully played the role. Sounds, doesn't it, like this major footballer was a non-believer and a non-card-bearing humanist?

.

Svend Robinson, the first openly gay member of the Canadian Parliament, is a non-theist. Sorry to report that, in what he has described as a moment of "utter irrationality," he pocketed an expensive piece of jewelry and has taken medical leave from his duties as an *MP*. He had been fighting for same-sex marriage, charter protection of gay rights and Palestinian autonomy.

.

"God Bless America," a favorite song of believers, was written by **Irving Berlin**. It now turns out that Berlin was an agnostic. In *Freethought Today* (Madison, Wisconsin, Freedom From Religion Foundation, May 2004) **Dan Barker** documents that Berlin, the son of a Jewish cantor, was an agnostic, that "patriotism was his religion." The song he wrote was a peace anthem, not a pro-war song as it sometimes now is performed. Also, his "White Christmas" was not about Christ but about the coming of a season.

In 1944 at a USO show in Chicago, just before I got shipped off to Omaha Beach, Berlin surprised a large group of us GIs with his unannounced appearance. He came onto the stage, dressed in an army uniform, and sang "Oh How I Hate To Get Up in the Morning," which originally he had composed in 1918 for a patriotic World War One show. Had I known about his agnosticism, I'd have tried to go backstage to show him my dog tags, which read that my religion was "None."

.

In June, a gay safari to Manhattan's Central Park Zoo was arranged to meet **Silo** and **Roy**, the two homosexual penguins that had been featured in *The Times*. Visitors saw them coo, cuddle and cavort.

Central Park had two other exhibitionists who recently performed. One was a 17-year-old schoolkid, the other his 32-year-old preoperative transsexual lover. Together they climbed 32 feet up a tree, shed all but their shorts, engaged in oral sex, refused to come down and taunted the police for more than three hours. When one cop gave them a shirt to cover up, the older of the two put it on, then dropped his underwear.

The boy's parochial school had kicked him out, the police

100

learned, and what triggered the event was that his mother was about to send him to a boarding school for unstable teens. From a prison psychiatric ward, the boy's lover exclaimed, "Over my dead body!" As I advised a visiting African who had just arrived as I was leaving, having shown him around the large park, "Be careful, it's a jungle out there!"

.

The star of *Jumpers* on Broadway is **Simon Russell Beale**, three-time Olivier winner in London. In an interview, and asked about his being gay, Beale said, "Just because I'm single [people] think I must be lonely. I'm not particularly. I'm sort of a gentleman who lunches."

.

All the following have something in common, but only one is peculiarly different from the rest: **Janet Jackson**, **Voltaire**, **Mazzini**, **Garibaldi**, **Haydn**, **Goethe**, **von Schiller**, **Benjamin Franklin**, **John Hancock**, **Paul Revere**, **George Washington**, and fourteen other presidents.

Jackson's recent clothing malfunction allegedly was accidental. But all the others were **Freemasons**, one of the secret lodge rituals of which is that of having each initiate expose his bare breast and his left leg, after which he is presented with a white cloth meant to symbolize innocence. The Grand Lodge of England dates back to 1723, when there were then thirty lodges.

The first in America was in 1730. Freemasonry rests upon deistic rituals, and to become a Mason one must say one believes in a Supreme Architect of the Universe. You don't have to define the phrase, so Jews, Christians and even humanists are known to have joined.

In 1738 **Pope Clement XII** issued a bull against any Catholic's joining the secret order, and under fascism and Nazism Freemasonry was forcibly eradicated in Italy, Austria and Germany. Today lodges are found from Iceland to Africa, India to Australia, Cuba to Japan, and all points in between. The basically deistic rituals are about ethical subjects and appeal, says a Manhattan wag, to rationalists and husbands eager to get away from the missus for a game of pool on a weekday night.

.

Many of us Yanks cannot believe the damage a religious Texan fundamentalist and his appointees have done to make our country so deeply divided in such a brief time! To hear them, either America is God's favored nation and we as a Christian country can do no wrong, or the country is an un-Christian pit of unrepentant sin, for which we are being punished.

Meanwhile, the majority of us feel a deep shame about the abuse of enemy prisoners, our leaders' arrogance, and their clear failure of leadership. In the November election, we'll do our damnedest to vote against the bad guys in the Executive and Legislative departments! Meanwhile, don't be surprised to hear that when we travel abroad for the rest of the year many of us are claiming to be Canadian.

.

"Go ahead, talk about same-sex marriage," observed a Manhattan wag. "Just give me plenty of some-sex marriage."

Autumn 2004

Marlon Brando was no stranger to sin so sweet. The sole time I saw him in person was in the 1960s at the **Bon Soir**, a Greenwich Village boîte, 40 West 8th Street, in New York City's Greenwich Village. Seated in a corner to the right of the stage, he was waiting for **Wally Cox** to perform.

But, first, a word about the allegedly Mafia-owned Bon Soir, which deserves never to be forgotten - it was a major nightclub that succeeded because of its early gay clientele and despite the time's abhorrence of homosexuality. Over the years it featured acts by **Kaye Ballard**, **Shirley Bassey**, **Phyllis Diller**, **Mike Nichols**, **Felicia Sanders**, **Barbra Streisand** and **Ethel Waters**.

The club was small. Lines often backed up for those wishing to stand at the bar. Waiters scrambled to serve food to those who had reservations at one of fewer than 25 small tables. At the bottom of the stairs, turn left to the restrooms or turn right to the fenced-off bar, which became so packed that hands touched hands, private parts and wallets, without anyone's being sure whose. The cognoscenti knew to slide their wallet into a stocking. Straights at the tables, who could not see over the waist-high wall at the bar, were oblivious as to what was going on.

A little sign atop each table told how much you would have to pay whether or not you ordered food or the several-drink minimum. It was wise to arrive early at either the first or second show of the evening, because the place's capacity was limited. And dark, this den of sophistication was so dark you wondered if

103

the walls were black or just in need of paint! The little light at the bar's cash register revealed what denomination of paper money standees had pulled out of their pocket. Once, I thought I'd given a ten but received change for a twenty. Once I thought I'd given a twenty but was told it was only a five. The bartender could have made a mint.

After an announcement about a "last call" for food service, the dimly lit room - entertaining mostly straight and extremely well-dressed couples at their tables - abruptly switched to entirely black, then onto the stage arrived m.c. **Jimmy Daniels**, a handsome gay black singer-actor who operated the tony club and was said to know, even to have "known," many of the city's wealthy and talented blacks and whites, not the least of whom were celebrated photographer **Carl Van Vechten**, who once had Daniels sit for a nude torso shot, and **Richmond Barthé**, who sculpted a marble portrait bust of him. Daniels not only performed but also kept the show moving along, usually introducing a comic, then a singer, then a group, another comic, and so forth.

Lighting was phenomenal. When **Kaye Ballard** or any other singer approached the end of a song, the spotlight was solely on the performer, its circular shape slowly diminishing until at the end note only the lighted head floated in black space - followed by three seconds of complete black, then up with the lights, and deafening applause!

Musical accompaniment usually was by the **Three Flames**, an all-black bass (**Avril Pollard**), piano (**Roy Testamark**), and guitar featuring **Tiger Haynes** (the Tin Man in the Broadway version of *The Wiz*). Cruisers who were three-deep at the bar focused on Tiger's tight pants as the big St Croix-born musician sat on a high stool, his trousers purposely failing to hide the merchandise. His pearly teeth and his consummate musicianship gained him much notoriety. "No, Mary," explained someone ingenuously at the all-male bar one night, " 'Big 10 Harmony' refers to the size of his *LP album*." The gossip was that, when in *New Faces of 1956* with drag queen **T. C. Jones**, Tiger had a white wife and, alas, was not bisexual.

The band became a key part of almost all the acts. When the full-bosomed five-by-five **Mae** "(I Ain't Gonna Be No) Topsy") **Barnes** attempted to slide up onto the grand piano's top but was far too overweight to manage, she'd exclaim, apologetically, "God damned Johnson Wax!" And Tiger would follow up with, "Sell it, Mae, don't give it away!"

Repartee between Tiger and **Phyllis Diller** seemed unrehearsed but was not. Her showbiz routine was to crab about her husband, cackle a loud laugh, then move to something timely. Notables were present every weekend, and one night there at a table and enjoying the many risqué jokes was California Senator **Richard M. Nixon**.

Unknown at the time, a young gal by the name of **Barbra Streisand** was paid $125 a week. She sang "Cry Me a River" and had everyone begging for encores. Another of her hits was "I Want to Be Bad," the words of which are quite tame by today's standards: "If it's naughty to rouge your lips, shake your shoulders, and swing your hips, let the lady confess, I want to be bad!"

Back to Brando. The night I saw him he was alone and greatly enjoying his drinks and himself, madly applauding after the Three Flames ended a tune and Daniels announced the next act. Out came **Wally Cox**, known as the bashful star of *Mr Peepers*, the 1952-5 television series. Wally's sad face evoked laughter, and his jokes came slowly, as if he had just thought them up. When the audience roared with laughter, gays at the bar always leading the group, Cox looked as if he were surprised he had been found to be so funny. And this made him seem even more lovingly wimpish.

At City College in New York, Cox had majored in botany and had become an actor only by accident. Whenever he uttered some kind of sarcastic comment, it seemed so out of place that even *that* was funny. Brando clapped loudly at all the right places, and the horned-rim-spectacle-wearing high-voiced Wally caught his eye several times. The two had been "roommates" at one point, Cox moving out allegedly because he couldn't put up with Marlon's pet raccoon. Gossips predicated other reasons, of course, and dozens of nocturnal carnivore-lovers were more than willing to move in with a newly lonesome, sexy Brando.

When Cox in 1973 died of a heart attack, Brando rushed from his Tahitian hideaway to arrange the cremation. Neither was a theist, and in a 1976 biography Brando was quoted as saying, "Like a large number of men, I, too, have had homosexual experiences, and I am not ashamed."

Overweight and at the end of his life wearing size 52 underwear, Brando died of lung failure on July 2, 2004. No public religious ceremony was performed for the acting giant who once refused to swear with an oath at his son's trial. "I will not swear on God because I don't believe in the conceptional sense and in this nonsense. What I will swear on is my children and my grandchildren."

[In February 2005, I received a message from the daughter of the Bon Soir's owner, Bronx-born **Nat Sackin** (1919 – 1982). **Ms. Lauren Sackin** came across this article and responded,

> It really captured the feeling of that era, and I enjoyed reading it very, very much. I was quite young at the time and remember it like it was just yesterday. Dark and smoky with the tinkle of glasses constantly. Believe it or not, with all the wonderful and awesome talent my dad had at the Bon Soir, it was the Coca-Colas and the turkey club sandwiches with Russian dressing that I remember enjoying the most (forgive me but I really was very young), although I do remember loving Phyllis Diller - she was so funny in this bizarre way and so ahead of her time. My goodness, if those walls could talk! Sadly, my dad is no longer with us. He died in 1982, but it is always heartwarming to read about The Bon Soir. I am sure he would have enjoyed your article as much as I did.

Her father, she wrote, was her hero, a veritable Greenwich Village denizen, very handsome, very articulate, and with a mysterious edge that women found undeniably attractive. Although raised in Fairlawn, New Jersey, she spent half her time in Greenwich Village, which was "awesomely beautiful then – still is – and always will be. I used to go to Washington Square Park all by myself, and no one ever bothered me."]

.

Gossip on the street, announced July 17 by **Ben Widdicombe** in New York's *Daily News*, is that a "gay Brando photo" is for sale, one showing Marlon on his knees "performing a sex act," allegedly on Mr Peepers. Possibly posed, but provocative to say the least, as was so much of Brando's dramatically rebellious life!

·

Ron Reagan Jr has told the press he is an atheist, not just a non-believer. The son of a US president, in a sharp dig at another son of a US president, is quoted as writing, "People who believe they are acting with the mandate of God, who see others who don't share their beliefs as inferior in the eyes of God, make dangerous leaders. Just ask **Osama Bin Laden**."

·

A member of the Democratic, not his father's Republican, Party, Ron spoke at the July Democratic National Convention against President **George W. Bush** and for embryonic-stem-cell research. Gays speculate as to when and where Reagan, who only recently mentioned his atheism, will come out of the closet as being bisexual.

·

Eric Douglas, 46, actor **Michael Douglas**'s youngest son, was found dead on July 6 after a long history of drug-taking. The press took note of his being Jewish and alarmingly overweight but did not mention he was gay.

·

Scottish actor and non-believer **Alan Cumming** claimed in July that if President Bush is re-elected, "I'm totally getting out of this country. I'm not going to want to be a citizen of this place."

Meanwhile, he is modeling **Gregory Sovell**'s C-In-2 line of briefs, which have a "sling support," an adjustable microfiber loop that is said to enhance "the male physique." What you see, as is well known, isn't always what you get!

Winter 2004

Cole Porter (1891-1964) is well known as the gay songwriter of "Begin the Beguine" (1935), "I've Got You Under My Skin" (1936), and "Night and Day" (1947). In 1919 he married his lifelong best friend, Linda Thomas, and they reportedly remained sexless together until her death in 1954. But was he a non-believer? Yes, according to ex-Christian **Dan Barker**, author of *Losing Faith in Faith: From Preacher to Atheist.*

In *Freethought Today*, Barker recounts how, when Porter was admitted to the hospital in 1964 and asked by a nurse filling out admittance forms about his religion, he replied, "Put down none." "Protestant?" asked the nurse. "Put down – none." Porter reiterated. **Robert Raison**, his friend, who had accompanied Porter, suggested that because he had been a Baptist why not put down Protestant? Cole refused, even when his condition had changed for the worse and he was near death.

"He was never a believer, and his several comments about his mother's attachments to Peru [Indiana] churches were dismissive." wrote biographer **William McBrien** (*Cole Porter*, 1998), which biographer and friend **George Eells** also reported, saying his mother went to church "to show off her new hats." At the age of 70, further documenting his non-theistic beliefs, Porter told his social secretary, **Mrs Everett W. Smith**, that he found no comfort "in trying to believe in a Supreme Being."

"You'd Be So Nice To Come Home To," he wrote for a dancer

and choreographer whom he had had a long romantic relationship with, **Nelson Barclift**. To Barclift, describing a religious feast of St Joseph he once had seen, Porter said he didn't have much use for such a day, that Joseph "resents being called the husband of the Virgin Mary & you know what she produced."

Porter also had infatuations and relationships with Russian dancer **Boris Kochno** and architect **Eddy Tauch**. His "Anything Goes" was strongly decried by churchgoers. In the 1930s, the Hayes Office, carrying out censorship guidelines, possibly led him to tone down the penultimate line of "Begin the Beguine" from "And we suddenly know the sweetness of sin" to "And we suddenly know what heaven we're in."

His 1953 *Can-Can* deliberately battled Puritanism, leading *The Catholic News* to deplore the scanty costumes worn by **Gwen Verdon**. But **Irving Berlin**, a fellow non-believer, wrote Porter that he had seen the show with his daughter, and "It's a swell show and I still say, to paraphrase an old barroom ballad, 'Anything I can do, you can do better'."

In his article entitled "Live and Let Live," Barker mentions that the 1946 movie of "Night and Day" starred "an uncomfortably miscast **Cary Grant** in a fanciful biopic that pointedly ignored the fact that the famous composer was notoriously gay." After seeing the film, Porter himself remarked, "It's a dream." When asked what kind of a dream, he replied, "I'd prefer not to say."

·

Santa Claus keeps arriving earlier. By October 25 he was urging everyone to max out their credit cards before Christmyth. On the airwaves, listeners again became the annual captive audience for "White Christmas" and "Jingle Bell Rock." Few, however, are aware that the composers of those two works were agnostics. **Irving Berlin** was not writing about a Christ but about the coming of a season. The rock song's lyrics were written by two unknowns: lyricist **Joe Beal** and composer **James Roth Boothe**. They came up with the unlikely hit in 1942 and were surprised that it became a hit in 1957.

My companion of 40 years, **Fernando Vargas**, was one of Boothe's recording engineers. Jim told the two of us vivid descriptions of his activities in public toilets, movie balconies, and The Rambles in Central Park. At Fernando's and my Variety Recording Studio in the 1970s, Jim once asked us to cash a thousand-dollar cheque representing royalties from Australia and New Zealand alone. Let's just say that the very successful Boothe, who died in 1977, was anything but a theist, but he did religiously get down prayer-like on his knees as often as he could . . . in bathhouse shower rooms.

.

Alexander, **Oliver Stone**'s $155-million film, is being praised by some as the "first honest portrayal of a gay historical figure." Gay critic **Steve Weinstein**, however, calls it *Alexander the Lousy*. He found the flick dull, "as though you've just sat through a three-hour community college Intro to Western Civ 101 lecture." In the "time-honored Hollywood tradition" of using British English to imply class, Philip is said to speak with a burr while Alexander uses American Standard Newscaster. And why does **Colin Ferrell**'s hair make him look "at various times like a street punk, Farrah Fawcett, Peter Frampton, and Hilary Clinton"? And why do the computer-simulated battle hordes look obviously phoney, and why is Alexander called "Great" at least four times - about 500 years before the name was coined - for starters? Weinstein also finds hilarious the scene in which Alexander comforts Hephaestion on his deathbed.

.

Far more gays are raving about *Kinsey*, starring **Liam Neeson** and directed by gay writer **Bill Condon**. In the first two minutes, the film begins mocking Christianity, shows a preacher who denounces modernity (zippers, telephones, electricity, and autos are claimed by him to have been spawned by Satan), and recounts how zoologist **Alfred Kinsey**, although raised a Methodist, never attended church.

The movie is consummately successful in showing how his 1948 and 1953 studies about sexual behavior turned America's sexual mores upside down. Sexual practices are talked about more directly than in any other movie that comes to mind, and Kinsey's visit to a gay bar to find some of the tens of thousands to be interviewed about their sexual practices is hilarious.

During the movie's opening week, the religious right screamed out against the portrayal of the atheistic Kinsey and all that he stood for. When you see the movie, don't leave before the end credits. Included is archival footage provided by the Kinsey Institute of copulating animals, including porcupines.

.

Several years before he died, I asked painter and fellow freethinker **Paul Cadmus** what Kinsey was like during the interview, one administered separately to his companion, photographer **Jared French**. It was strictly business, very thorough, statistics-gathering, he told me - the first orgasm, the size of the penis when flaccid and when erect, how much activity per week, etc. And did he think Kinsey was gay? Yes, Cadmus thought he probably was, and this was before it was generally known that Kinsey had had homosexual experiences.

.

Alan Cumming, who starred on Broadway in *Cabaret*, is the freethinker whose fragrance - appropriately priced at $69 for a 3.4-ounce bottle and called Cumming - will go on sale in February. It's the ideal gift for those who'd like squirts of Cumming all over their bodies.

.

Not to change the subject, according to **Michael Musto** in *Village Voice*, **Gore Vidal** once observed in some unknown context that "Boys are expected to squirt as often as possible in order to fructify an egg."

Spring 2005

America's White House, it now appears, has been home to two presidents who allegedly were not straight. **James Buchanan** (1791 - 1868), the only unmarried one, at times was derisively called "Miss Nancy" by some. He shared rooms with an associate, Alabama Senator **William Rufus de Vane King** and, when they separated, wrote, "I am selfish enough to hope you will not be able to procure an associate who will cause you to feel no regret at our separation." Elsewhere, he once went on record that "I have seldom met an intelligent person whose views were not narrowed and distorted by religion." In politically Puritan America, understandably, he remained a nominal Presbyterian.

Abraham Lincoln (1809 – 1865), the founder of our majority party - the Republican, that is now headed by George W. Bush - shared a double bed for four years with 23-year-old **Joshua Fry Speed**. Many writers, including **Larry Cramer** and **Gore Vidal**, have long speculated about Lincoln's sex life. This I reported in my summer 1998 column.

Now in 2005, *The Intimate World of Abraham Lincoln* (Free Press), by sex researcher **C. A. Tripp,** contends that Lincoln had attachments to men from his youth to his presidency. Tripp, who once worked with **Alfred Kinsey**, has collected a mountain of material and alleges that Lincoln suffered from depression when, after four years together, Speed moved. Lincoln wrote, "I am now the most miserable man living." Also, Tripp documents that a young Lincoln bed-shared with **Billy Greene**, who wrote that Lincoln's "thighs were as perfect as a human being could be." Another bed-sharer, **Captain David Derickson**, used Lincoln's night shirt on occasions when Mrs Lincoln was not home. Tripp lays out an exhaustive amount of revealing details in his convincing work.

Tripp's research is pseudoscientific, say conservative critics, his conclusions based upon highly circumstantial evidence. In frontier times men often slept in the same bed, they counter, pointing out that the **Marquis de Lafayette** and **George**

Washington curled up together, exhausted, during the Battle of Monmouth – those were the days when the Frenchman helped us fight the British, who may or may not have been bed-sharers, or even German mercenaries.

One should not call Lincoln gay, a word not used until recently, and homosexuality didn't find its way into print in English until 1892 or so. Thus, Lincoln's sexual orientation is questionable. This leads one to wonder if the next exposé will be that scandalmongers were right about Washington, the childless "father of his country," whose secret love might have been Treasury Secretary **Alexander Hamilton**. Suffice it to say that Lincoln at the very least may have been bi-sexual in his feelings, maybe even in practice.

Secretive and unconventional in many ways, Lincoln despite pressures of the time remained unchurched. **William Herndon**, Lincoln's law partner, close friend, and biographer, wrote that Lincoln liked the writings of **Thomas Paine** and habitually denied the supernatural birth of Jesus. In one of his books, in fact, he had changed *John* 16:27 from "Ye have loved me, and have believed that I came from God" to "from nature," illustrating his deistic, not theistic, stance.

．

Three noted freethinkers have recently died: playwright **Arthur Miller** (straight, 89); architect **Philip Johnson** (gay, 98); and critic **Susan Sontag** (gay, 71).

My memories about Miller, with whom I worked on the original Broadway production of *After the Fall*, can be found online - http://wasm.us - as well as copies of our correspondence and my dishing the dirt about **Marilyn Monroe** (had a cute little mole betwixt her boobs). He refused to declare himself about his philosophic outlook, but I found him not to be a dues-paying humanist of any stripe. Rather, he was a humanities humanist, like so many freethinkers found in my *Celebrities in Hell*.

．

Philip Johnson, the American dean of architects, died in his Glass House, a cube with a compound that included an all-brick guest house that he built in New Canaan, Connecticut, and shared with **David Whitney**. Their neighbor for three decades, I never knew Johnson was gay, partly because he lived in town on weekends and I lived weekends in New York City. Although he received barbs about his Seagram Building, the AT&T Tower with a Chippendale top, and a Cathedral of Hope in Dallas for a gay congregation, he knew how to dish. His contemporary, **Frank Lloyd Wright**, he quipped, was "the greatest architect of the 19th century."

During a house tour arranged by a garden club decades ago, Johnson asked me my occupation, and I replied that at the moment I was teaching **Bertrand Russell**'s *Why I Am Not A Christian*. Having majored in Greek at Harvard, he knew Russell's work well, so I asked if he was a naturalist. He said something to the effect that the word had many meanings but that he was no supernaturalist. "And when are you going to build a house in New Canaan that a teacher can afford?" He laughed loudly.

Johnson told writers **Hilary Lewis** and **John O'Connor**, "My philosophical outlook dates from a time and a way of thinking that differs from the liberal, acceptable, politically correct line that we all subscribe to today. To me, **Plato** was the worst – living the good and the true and the beautiful. There's no such thing as the good or the true or the beautiful. I'm a relativist. I'm a nihilist." He disliked "spiritual" as a concept, saying of his celebrated gay church, "I love cathedrals, even though I'm not religious."

"I like the thought that what we are to do on this earth is embellish it for its greater beauty . . . so that oncoming generations can look back to the shapes we leave here and get the same thrill that I get in looking back at theirs - at the Parthenon, at Chartres Cathedral."

As for his having flirted in the 1930s with right-wing politics and Hitler-style fascism and anti-Semitism in Berlin, in later years he apologized publicly: "I have no excuse [for] such utter, unbelievable stupidity. I don't know how you expiate guilt." One Manhattan wag has speculated that he was never as interested in the philosophy of fascism as in the anatomy of young uniformed Nazi soldiers.

·

Obituaries for critic and intellectual **Susan Sontag** extensively covered her life, but few except for *The Economist* and New York's *Daily News* mentioned that famed photographer **Annie Leibovitz** had been her companion for 20 years. *The New York Times* in its 4,000-word front-page story made no such mention, claiming later that neither Ms. Leibovitz nor Ms. Sontag's son, **David Rieff**, would confirm any relationship. Meanwhile, no one mentioned that Sontag once wrote, "Religion is probably, after sex, the second oldest resource which human beings have available to them for blowing away their minds."

·

Two of today's most popular TV stars, both gay and strikingly handsome, are CNN's **Anderson Cooper** (son of Gloria Vanderbilt and the late Wyatt Cooper) and WABC-TV's weatherman **Sam Champion**. Neither has professed being a member of any organized religion, and both avoid labels. When the ball drops in Times Square on New Year's Eve, it will be CNN's platinum-haired Cooper who will host the program.

.

In a blow-by-blow account, New York journals have reported a local rabbi's prickly problem with authorities. Not content with performing genital mutilation on a baby, he used the technique of stopping the bleeding by sucking its penis, thereby giving the kid herpes. It's not clear if the rabbi, whose congregation knew about his favorable reputation for doing such, is protected under a religious cloak, or even if he was wearing one.

Paul Cadmus (1904—1999)

Paul Cadmus (l.) with the author

Paul Cadmus, the controversial painter of "The Fleet's In!" and "The Seven Deadly Sins," became a distinguished member of the American Academy of Arts and Letters in 1974. In 1984, he was the subject for a video-recording, "Paul Cadmus, Enfant Terrible at 80." At the time, a *New York Times* reviewer noted,

> Recent interest in representational painting has fostered an appreciation of artists whose realist modes, long out of the stylistic and commercial mainstreams, are now receiving renewed attention. . . . For Mr. Cadmus, best known for his earlier, more accessible works, including the much reproduced New York street and restaurant scenes and Coney Island panoramas, also practices a dark, more personal, visionary magic realism in which black humor and distant allusions are endemic.

Cadmus and an early lover, painter **Jared French**, spent time on the island of Majorca, where he painted "Shore Leave" and "YMCA Locker Room." His circle included **Christopher Isherwood**, **W. H. Auden**, **George Balanchine**, **George Platt**

Lynes, **George Tooker**, **Lincoln Kirstein** (the husband of his sister **Fidelma**), and **E. M. Forster**.

He was unsure about his ancestry: "I think my ancestors sailed from Jutland (Denmark) around 1710. My father's side may have been Dutch and, like Erasmus, Latinized the name. My mother, conceived in Spain, was born in New York. Her father was Basque, her mother Cuban. Maybe I was just a cad to begin with," he joked, "and the name was Latinized."

His parents, both artists, encouraged their son and their daughter, Fidelma, to study art, and Cadmus began with an interest in antiques. One day at the National Academy of Design in uptown Manhattan and, knowing that older art students had nude models to work with, he peered through a peephole and saw a naked female. "I had never seen a stranger in the nude. It was a revelation," he told journalist **Richard Goldstein**. Naked men would follow. It was the start of his becoming the artist who painted the male body with more sensuality, Goldstein observed (*Village Voice*, 18 May 1999), than any American artist of the century:

> "The Fleet's In!" [is] the 1934 painting that made him an art star. In this knowing study of carousing sailors, there are not only buns and baskets on proud display but loose ladies admiring the briny trade and even a fey gentleman offering a cigarette to an eager gob. The navy was not amused. An outraged admiral had the painting removed before it could be shown at the Corcoran Gallery in Washington, D.C. A sequel, "Sailors and Floosies" (1938), featuring the angelic seaman in slumber, grasping his crotch, fared no better in San Francisco; "in the interest of national unity," it was taken off the wall.

In "Shore Leave" (1933), a gay man is clearly propositioning a willing sailor, but what one notices first is the ripe women in the foreground and a recumbent swab with his bulging crotch in full view. Sometimes the queers come out to play, as in "Fantasia on a Theme by Dr. S." (1946), which is set on Fire Island. But usually the artist's eye is drawn to what is often ignored in modern painting: a casually muscled male physique and an utterly open attitude. Looking at this pantheon of locker-room studs, seafood Sampsons, and young waifs lounging in the playground with baseball bats jammed between their legs, one sees a quality beyond the ideologically mandated worship of the working class. Call it longing.

"I was fascinated by the sailors, and I used to sit on a bench and watch them all the time," Cadmus recalls. In fact, Riverside Park around 96th Street was a prime cruising ground in the 1930s, largely because it was where the warships docked. "The uniforms were so tight and form-fitting that they were an inspiration. I was young enough to be propositioned by the sailors, who would offer to take me back to the boat, but I never went. They were too unattractive, or maybe I was too timid. I don't know."

"The male nude has been a specialty of my own oeuvre," Cadmus agreed, "when I am not being concerned with the foibles of people in daily life: men, women, and children. . . . We are made, we are told, 'in God's image,' and we assume that He was not clothed by Armani or Brooks Brothers or, if He is She, not attired by Balenciaga or Donna Karan."

In 1992, Lincoln Kirstein, the founding director of the New York City Ballet, wrote a definitive study, *Paul Cadmus*, which described his relationship with other artists and writers, including W. H. Auden. While posing for a portrait, E. M. Forster was said to have passed the time reading aloud passages from *Maurice*. Kirstein described Cadmus's work as being "executed with the technical virtuosity and anatomical precision of the Renaissance masters that celebrate the beauty of the human body." Agreeing, **Guy Davenport** in an introduction for *The Drawings of Paul Cadmus* (1989) stated that "Not since Michelangelo has any artist done so many studies of the male nude." He included dozens of such examples.

> Cadmus, who in 94 years completed over 120 paintings, delighted in such observations. "I do love Michelangelo's male forms," he has said, adding that "Michelangelo's women often look like males with grapefruits attached." "It seems that genitalia," Cadmus lamented about the public taste, "equal pornography." But not for him personally: "My penis is not the most important organ in my body. My eyes are."

In 1989, during a discussion about philosophy, Cadmus asked me what I meant by "humanism," and I mentioned that when I was **Lionel Trilling**'s student in the 1940s I had found seven different humanisms: (1) lexicographical humanism, denoting devotion to human interests; (2) the ancient humanism represented by such as **Democritus** and **Lucretius**; (3) classical humanism, such as the views of **Erasmus** and **More**; (4) theistic humanism, such as that of **Maritain**, with its supernaturalistic overtones; (5) atheistic humanism, including **Sartre**'s existentialism; (6) communistic humanism, for **Karl Marx** had been a naturalist who at first had called his outlook "a new humanism," and **Fidel Castro** who had once called his philosophic outlook "humanism"; and (7) naturalistic humanism, the term made popular by **Corliss Lamont** and others, later called secular humanism.

> Your request should have a worthy answer but it would take me days to try to compose one (as I used to do when I first began writing to E. M. Forster). The subject is too complicated for this feeble old mind to go into deeply. The simple description of a humanist is one who is interested in humans (not as profound as the *Oxford Universal Dictionary's* definition, "a student of human affairs, or of human nature").
>
> I'm no student. I guess I somewhat fit in Naturalistic Humanism #7.

Later, in an interview at his Connecticut home, Cadmus discussed religion and his increased interest in the philosophy of naturalistic humanism, which we both came to agree should more aptly be termed "humanistic naturalism," the emphasis being upon naturalism, the qualifier being a reference to the humanities. We also agreed that the International Academy of Humanism was woefully and surprisingly deficient in its numbers of artists and musicians. On another occasion, he met **Anita Weschler**, sculptor of "The Humanist" [which is at the Institute for Humanist Studies in Albany, New York]. "We have much in common," he told the fellow nonagenarian. "We're both humanistic naturalists!"

"I've always liked the story of the Albigensians," Cadmus mused, "who were besieged by the Pope at Beziers. His soldiers asked him: 'How do we know the heretics from the Christians?' The Pope replied, 'Burn them all. God will know his own.' " A devout Catholic until he was seventeen, he then "shed it all."

Cadmus is cited by **Charles Kaiser** in *The Gay Metropolis 1940 —1996* (1997) as having painted key individuals and scenes of that period. Kaiser noted that Cadmus met **Jon Andersson**, 27, when he himself was 59 and "I never wanted to be with anyone else." That included the time he was invited to a long-ago party by **Truman Capote**. Capote's long-time companion **Jack Dunphy** told him he could not bring a male guest, that "Truman said he didn't want to ask 'a bunch of fags' to his party." This infuriated Andersson and was one of the few times the two did not appear together in public or private. At a book signing when Kaiser referred to Cadmus as the only artist to draw so many male nudes, the then ninety-two-year-old quipped, "Well, there was **Michelangelo**."

Kaiser quotes Cadmus as having been interviewed by **Alfred Kinsey**: "He took homosexuality just as calmly as he did his work with wasps. He interviewed me about my sex life–how many orgasms, how big it was, measure it before and after." Kinsey even went to dinner at Cadmus's house following the interview.

December 1st, at the D. C. Moore Gallery in New York City, Cadmus celebrated his 95th birthday two weeks early. At that event, several hundred friends gathered, and Cadmus was hale, hearty, and on his feet greeting everyone. "He's another of us humanistic naturalists," Cadmus said to a fellow member of the Academy, **Chuck Close**, introducing me. In an adjacent room, a large, humorous painting he had entitled "A Study of David and Goliath" showed Jon holding Cadmus's head on a platter. Fortunately, the birthday party was held early. He died five days before his 95th birthday.

Gay in the 1960s
[Written in June 2003 – published in New York City's Greenwich Village *Villager*]

It was the best of times. It was the worst of times.

Gay life in the 1960s was, for sure, an entirely different time, a time in which falling in love monthly, or even weekly, was neither impossible nor improbable.

It was a dangerous time, however, to be openly gay. Physicians who cured our venereal diseases scolded us for having done what we did to get sick. Psychiatrists ruled that we were mentally sick. Neighbors maliciously gossiped about who was visiting late last night. Landlords asked gay couples, hoping to rent, if they were related. Monotheists called us sinners, threatening that if we didn't choose to be heterosexual we would not get to Heaven (making that theological invention all the more undesirable). If we were slightly on the fey side, we could get a black eye, a bloody lip or worse. Sometimes, in self-defense, we related antigay jokes to throw people off.

Even if we carefully stayed in the closet, it was difficult to play The Majority's game. When I was an acting first sergeant in charge of a company that landed on Omaha Beach in 1944, I did play the game, difficult as it was. Although I preferred music, art, poetry and ballet to sports, I guarded against expressing myself. Whenever I got a leave during the time I was in the Army, I chose to travel alone. Who better than gays to understand Stevenson's "The Strange Case of Dr. Jekyll and Mr. Hyde"!

In 1969, Vice President Spiro Agnew would have become president if Richard Nixon had died. Katharine Hepburn and Barbra Streisand tied as best actresses for an Oscar. "1776" and "The Great White Hope" won Antoinette Perry awards. Billie Jean King was one of the top tennis players. If treated, gonorrhea, syphilis and other venereal diseases were not life threatening. It cost 20 cents to ride the subway.

Sex in New York City was readily available, night and day. The Rambles in Central Park was one place where openly gay male sex occurred and allegedly had ever since the William Cullen Bryant-inspired area first opened. All that shrubbery, all those dark places in which to hide and to meet....

Many small parks had gay meeting spots, and all large parks had cruising areas. Brooklyn's Prospect Park had several busy sites. Riverside Drive's area stretched from the Soldiers and Sailors Monument to General Grant's Tomb and on up past Harlem. Parks along the East River and areas near the Battery were places to hook up. The park at Washington Sq. was appealing, particularly the northwest corner where guys leaned suggestively on the railings. If anyone asked the time, he really was inviting you to his nearby apartment. Rendezvous were followed by an exchange of names and phone numbers — wrong numbers, of course, if either thought he might do better falling in love after a one-night stand with someone else tomorrow.

The subway during rush hour could be particularly erotic. Today, eyes that focus on your midsection are searching out your billfold, but since 1948 as soon as I arrived in the city I understood that any such glance was being made for another reason.

Park and subway toilets were busy places. In some, a noisy door when opened alerted everyone inside to stop for a moment to make sure the newcomer was not a cop in uniform. Cops not in uniform were the problem, for they enjoyed being the bait, then handing out a ticket (and maybe upon arriving at court receiving

$400 to forget details so that the judge would throw the case out).

Brando and Mr. Peepers

Coffee houses, museums, department stores, the opera, the ballet, the symphony, bathhouses like the Everard, bars like Mary's on Eighth St. and the Cork Club on W. 72nd, or nightclubs like the Bon Soir on Eighth St. (where Marlon Brando could be seen applauding Mr. Peepers, his boyfriend Wally Cox),

Also, there was a place such as the Oscar Wilde Memorial Bookshop, the first of its kind openly displaying books by and about homosexuals. All were places one might fall in love, whether for a short time. Or, in my case, for four memorable, truly love-filled decades.

Favorites for many gays were the movie houses on The Deuce: the Victory, Lyric, Times Square, Apollo, Selwyn, New Amsterdam, Liberty, Empire, and the Harris. But away from 42nd St. were many other houses where people came to see people, not the movie: the huge Adonis near Eighth Ave. and 55th; the smallish Roxy in Greenwich Village; the crumbling Metropolitan on W. 14th; and the busiest place in Manhattan, Variety Photoplays on Third Ave. just off 14th Street. Drawn to such places by word-of-mouth - no guidebooks were available - were many who had escaped from homophobic small towns across the country, people eager to meet and be met, all dependent upon the kindness of strangers.

At the western end of Christopher St., it was not easy to be rejected, particularly if someone liked your physique, your manner, or simply your attitude. During the evenings, dark areas in the Village tended to attract numbers of people. A few blocks uptown from Christopher, unlocked and parked semi-trailer containers became known as "the trucks," and dozens of all sizes and varieties of men desperately fought to get packed into the relatively small wooden containers' darkness, where anonymous sex was commonplace.

The gay bar in the 1960s that became known around the world as a human rights symbol was the Stonewall Inn. On a Friday night, 27 June 1969, a major struggle that had been developing internationally for years has been described in Vern Bullough's *Before Stonewall*.

My recollection of the bar itself was that it was dingy. Upon entering, you signed a book with a name (seldom your own), paid $3 to cover two watered down $1 drinks, and found a place to stand or someone who wanted to dance. It was illegal for men to dance with men, although women could dance with women. To gay teenagers, the place was like a refuge, a site where they could choose the music and could dance with those they chose. Stories abounded that violence was always present in the allegedly Mafia-owned and operated bars. However, one reliable source told me he knew the two who rented the place, saying, perhaps naively in light of the facts, that they were simply young Italian entrepreneurs, that not all Italians are connected with the Mafia. At least the bar was there for all of us to enjoy with our fellow outlaws.

The rebellion begins...

Because of the underage customers, the prevalence of drugs, and the possibility of illegal dancing or other acts, the police went openly to gay bars, including for payoffs. On this Friday night, however, a few of the employees began to be arrested. Some customers were told to leave but others were detained. The raid turned ugly around 2 a.m. Although perhaps a hundred or so were involved that night, many more hundreds of contradictory "Rashomon"-like versions can be found as to what actually happened. Angry patrons, both inside and outside, are said to have started yelling "Gay Power," throwing stones, coins and bottles. Not all onlookers were pleased with seeing such civil disobedience, and some are said to have thrown bottles at the gays. On one of the nights, the cops barricaded themselves inside because the place was attacked from outside by several hundred. Trapped, the cops called for reinforcements. But when the media reported the escalating and eye-catching happening, the word got around fast, and hundreds returned the following nights.

As the past treasurer of two different Stonewall veterans' groups, both now extinct, I conducted many person-to-person interviews with individuals I trusted to honestly express their experiences. One, Danny (who now is a corporate suit and might not want his last name included) was among the most credible. He had no vested interest in exaggerating or lying. In fact, he stopped paying dues, like others who became critical of some of the egomaniacal leaders of the several fissiparous Stonewall veterans' groups.

When I interviewed Danny five years ago and posted his memories on the Web, he recalled to me that in 1967 he was amazed to find guys dancing with guys at the Stonewall. In any of the bars, you could not stand at the bar with your back to it, or it would be considered soliciting and the bar could be shut down. Also, you could not touch when dancing.

"Back in 1969," Danny said, "I was a hippie on my way to the Stonewall to go dancing with my friend Keith, who was home from college for summer break. Keith and I were talking about the revolution that would be coming along some day. We thought that the Young Lords, or the Black Panthers, would start it. We had no idea of gay rights. We were both 20 and the world was changing so fast. There was now a women's movement, and Vietnam was still going on. Early that year in March there was the first 'be-in' at Grand Central Station, with about 400 to 500 young people smoking pot and singing folk songs and antiwar songs. The police raided the be-in and hit many a young person with their clubs, pulling us by our long hair into the paddy wagons. Many of the people there were gay. Because of the times and the antiwar movement, most young gay people had experiences with demonstrations. The only gay movement that I knew of at the time was the Mattachine Society, and those people were over 30 . . . and most of us didn't trust anyone over 30!

"As Keith and I arrived, the police cars and paddy wagon were already at the bar. It was not uncommon for gay bars to be raided. The people started yelling at the cops and throwing pennies at them. Around the corner on Seventh Ave. was a new building being constructed, and someone ran and got bricks from there and started throwing them at the police. The cops went wild! There was no way to contain the crowd because of the location of the bar. You could run down West Fourth, Seventh Avenue, Waverly Place, or Christopher St., and still end up back at the bar."

Danny's recollections were identical to my own, for I was present the second night (Saturday, June 28). Many of us did not know about the raid the night before. We were simply part of a happening, not participants in what turned out to be an important historic event. Nevertheless, a larger crowd showed up. According to Danny, "We decided to liberate the bar and reopen it so we could dance. I really don't think any of us thought that this was the start of the gay rights movement. Someone got a parking meter and smashed open the bar doors. More cops were called in. The riot started again and garbage cans were set on fire, Molotov cocktails were thrown and it was like a war zone! The thing was that because of the night before we as gay people discovered that we would stand up and fight together, something we never knew before. We were so fragmented when it came to our own rights." I had been one of those across the street who had thrown a garbage container, then had run like hell to escape from a cop who came after me.

Danny's other recollections jibe with my own: "The Stonewall was a great place if you were young and gay. Many nights I did the Jerk or the Boston Monkey or some latest line-dance craze till the bar closed. I hung out with a lot of people who worked there. Barbara Eden who worked the coat check was a good friend of mine, and I dated Frankie who worked the front door and was sometimes a bartender there. The Stonewall changed with the times. As the '60s progressed they put in black lights and Day-Glo posters. The lover I had at the time, George, sold acid there. Let's face it: the place was Mafia-owned!

"One myth that seems to have grown about the riot was that drag queens started it," Danny continued. "That's not true. There were what we called a lot of Flame Queens there. A Flame Queen wore hip huggers, Tom Jones shirts, and maybe eye makeup. They would tease up their hair and were very effeminate, like Emory in "Boys in the Band." Most young people's clothes at the time had become pretty asexual. You could not be in full drag at the time. You had to have three articles of men's clothing on or you would be arrested for impersonating a woman. Most people were into dressing the new style, unisex.

"We Stonewall vets were just a bunch of kids, not heroes," Danny continued. "We simply wanted to dance and not be harassed. No one knew that that night would be thought of as the start of the gay movement. My own heroes are people like you who started G.L.F. [Gay Liberation Front] and G.A.A. [Gay Activists Alliance]. You people were the real movers and shakers."

No one took photos

The trouble continued through Thursday, July 3. At Fedora's, another refuge, drinkers at the bar and diners in what is one of Manhattan's oldest family-owned restaurants (owned and operated 51 years now by Fedora Dorato) have traded for decades the various versions of what happened. Unfortunately, the rebellion was neither photographed nor professionally documented. Some versions of what happened, however, can be found in Martin Duberman's *Stonewall* (1994), which became the basis for a 1996 movie with the same title. Randy Wicker, the "atheist priest," co-authored with Kay Tobin "The Gay Crusaders," which contains interviews with other Stonewallers. Stormé DeLarverie was the subject of a 1987 film, "Stormé: The Lady of the Jewel Box." Look for a forthcoming book, *Stonewall, The Riots That Sparked The Gay Revolution* by the historian David Carter. [Although I supplied material, he failed to credit me. It's still a good resource book.]

The sign above the bar at the Stonewall